# MOM, TAKE TIME

**Pat A. Baker**

**BAKER BOOK HOUSE**
**Grand Rapids, Michigan**

Because they took time to introduce me to
the purpose in living through Christ,
I dedicate this book to my parents
LAWRENCE W. HOFFMEISTER
and
LORENE MABREY HOFFMEISTER

Copyright 1976 by
Pat Baker

Seventh printing, March 1989

Additional copies may be ordered from the author at
214 West Summit, Bolivar, MO  65613

Printed in the United States of America

# PREFACE

*"Train up a child in the way he should go and when he is old he will not depart from it"* Prov. 22:6.

How does a mother feel the first time the nurse places her baby in her arms? No mother has dreamed the same dreams, or thought of the same ways to discipline, to comfort, or to provide. None of them has even prayed the same prayers. But all mothers share a common bond when it comes to the gift of time. There is allotted to everyone the same amount of time —time to grow a family. It does not matter how the world looks at a mother: what she does with her child, or how it judges whether she is a good or bad mother. But it does matter what actually goes on behind the doors of her world-at-home.

This book has one purpose—to share with each mother how vital it is to *take time* with her children in a world that clamors for her quality time doing lesser things.

I feel deeply that the basic essentials of proper development are mental, physical, spiritual, and so-cial. The basis of this belief comes from Jesus' own development: "And Jesus increased in wisdom and in stature and in favor with God and man" (Luke 2:52).

Of equal importance is the fact that a mother must find time for herself. She is an individual, too. She will need to find healthy ways of releasing the pressures she feels as a mother. She will want to continue to take pride in her physical appearance and never stop finding refreshing ways of developing her mental growth. It is not enough that she feed and care for her family; she must also feed and care for her soul. Meditation times are hard to find, but there are ways. The suggestions in this book show ways that have been effective for other mothers.

The postlude has been written for husband and wife to share together. It is written in the belief that they must take time for each other to avoid the prospects of getting into a parent trap of not having time for each other as they engage in rearing their family together.

Time. How do you plan to use it with your family, mom?

## A Note to Dad

Although mom is the main character in this book, I would like to emphasize that you should take time to have the same meaningful experiences with your child. When he has had a new learning situation during the day, let your wife share it with you; then engage yourself in a similar situation with him.

You may feel it is impossible to find the energy, after a day's work, to play and learn with your child. But it can be done—it must be done. Remember, dad, take time.

# CONTENTS

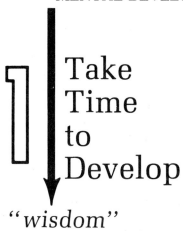

# Take Time to Develop

## *"wisdom"*

"Mom, I have things in my brain. There are lots of rooms. People are the size of ants. I have one large room, but I can't tell anyone what's in it!" Does our five-year-old mean this room holds her secrets or is it a room to be filled and satisfied with her curiosities as she reaches various stages of her mental growth? "Get wisdom, get understanding: forget it not; neither decline from the words of my mouth" (Prov. 4:5).

It will take time to help your child develop mentally. Take time to talk with him; encourage him. Speak to him by using positive words. Negativism will slow down his learning. Take time to respond to all the emotions he will experience. Help him work through his problems successfully, no matter how small they may seem to you. Be determined never to get too busy to know your child. Live closely with him and learn with him. Use every technique to make your child's learning gratifying.

The attitudes you have from the time of his birth will have a lasting influence on his interests and motivations. Until he is four years old, he will imitate you and other adults. You will become his standard.

He will imitate your voice, language habits, attitudes, and emotions.

Mom, pursue knowledge, get excited about it, and your child will be motivated to learn. Whatever you have to say can make the thought of learning thrilling or boring, interesting or tedious, fascinating or dull.

Stimulate his learning. Don't leave it to chance. Plan, discuss, explore, experience, and carry out every day's procedure for learning. Take time to talk and read with your child. Expose him to adult conversation; include him in family plans. Shop together, eat out, visit parks, and see animals at the zoo. Give him time to wonder about the snow, trees, and flowers. Be interested in discovering things with your child. Mom, it is going to take time to develop your child's mental abilities.

# INFANCY

How do you begin developing the mentality of an infant? The most important way is to establish security with your baby. Before he can learn, his basic needs must be satisfied. Holding him when you feed him, and responding when he is uncomfortable are simple daily tasks during his first days. When his security has been established, he will begin interacting and learning from his surroundings.

From birth each different sound your baby hears or object he sees, touches, tastes, and smells will be new. One of the first ways to arouse his senses is to expose him to sounds, specially human talk. Introduce him to colors by placing above his crib brightly colored mobiles which he may attempt to grab. He may even react to light or a pattern before his eyes. Make objects available for him to feel, such as satin trim on his blanket, smooth rattles, and soft balls. Remember two things here: different textures will mean different things to him, and toys must be his size. Finally, open new tastes and smells to him in a natural way by introducing new foods. All of these experiences stimulate his senses and help his intellectual progress.

At six months of age he should be able to sit in a car seat comfortably. Over and over again, as you travel, show him objects—trees, animals, cars, houses, flowers, and rocks. Repetition is good for learning.

It is important for him to hear stories. It stirs the imagination, involves hearing, seeing, and thought. Have a variety of stories and primary song books. At age two he will begin enacting some of the simple stories you have read. He will become "mom," "dad," or animals. Blocks will become trains; dolls will become live babies.

Prepare a search game. Have him follow a toy through several hiding places. This will build his memory.

He is now ready for a peg board. This one toy stimulates sound, touch, sight, and disappearing objects. He can now differentiate between triangular, circular, and square blocks. Many educational toys can be purchased that teach these shapes.

By three years of age he can beat a fairly good rhythm. You can teach him the difference between high and low notes, slow and fast rhythms, and loud and soft intensities. Beverly recorded music on a cassette player for her children when they were very young. She chose a range of music from children's musicals, to stringed ensembles, to Handel's *Messiah*. Many of these songs became their favorites.

Every activity you produce may seem elementary and unimportant to you; but as you perform with your baby, watch him achieve. And remember—his first four years of life are crucial in building the foundation to help him reach his intellectual potential. You have started him well by seeing the importance of small basic beginnings.

# PRESCHOOL

Take time to read to your preschooler. Introduce

him to a world of good literature. Help him begin his own personal library and add to it through the years. As you read to him, speak with expression. This type of reading aloud makes his mental powers alert and puts his imagination into action.

Tell make-up stories. Vary the procedure. Instead of you telling a complete story, stop at certain points and let your child add a short portion of the story; then you finish it.

Call the public library to see if it offers a weekly children's story hour. Buy activity books that suggest word search, hidden objects, ways to use numbers and recognize quantities.

If you are making a trip, start a simple game with road signs and billboards. If you have taught your child the alphabet, you can have fun with letters. Have him spell the large bold words on road signs. Tell him what the words spell. He will not only be learning to spell, but he will be learning to observe highway rules. Have him find an *a* on the first billboard, on the next one a *b*, going through the alphabet in this manner. Incidentally, this is an excellent way to help the miles go by quickly on a long trip.

During late preschool, use a story book that has a certain word in it several times. Go through the pages slowly and have him search for the word. A variation of this is to cut out or circle a short paragraph in a magazine or newspaper. Choose a vowel and have him circle it each time it appears.

This is an excellent time for you and your husband to begin saving for a set of encyclopedias. The *Child Craft* book set, published by Field Enterprises Educational Corporation, is also an excellent teaching resource center. This set contains poetry, fairy and animal stories, stories of famous men and children from other countries, types of creative play and hobbies, and articles on science and art and music. Three of the books deal with family living and another book discusses the school-age child. These books are invaluable and can be at your disposal every day. Make books an important part of your child's development.

There are a variety of activities you can present to sharpen the senses of your curious preschooler. Place a cottonball and a rock on a tray, then an orange and an apple, and finally a coarse piece of sandpaper and a soft fabric. Have him touch the first two and ask, "Which one is hard and which one is soft?" "Which one is bumpy and which one is smooth?" "Which one is rough and which one is soft?" It is very important for him to feel an object in order to comprehend it. Let him handle, feel the texture, and explore the surface of each object.

For taste use the same procedure with opposites: sweet-sour, hot-cold, soft-hard. Test his sense of smell. Let him smell different odors, such as onion, lemon, cinnamon, bread, fruit, and vegetables. Then blindfold him and have him smell each item and try to distinguish each odor.

He can learn certain parts of his body by this simple verse:

> I touch my hair, my nose, my eyes.
> I sit up straight and then I rise.
> I touch my ears, my mouth, my chin.
> And quietly sit down again.

Use variations with this. Say it slow, fast, soft, loud. See if he can sit down without making a noise.

For hearing, use musical records or a piano. Have him feel the rhythm by stamping, marching, clapping, or swaying. Give him a head scarf and let him move around the room, using actions to set his own musical mood.

For seeing, point to objects around the house or outdoors and encourage him to tell you the names of each thing. Take him to a museum, a historical site, or a botanical garden. Observe what interests him, and then later read and discuss at length new ideas each of these presents.

Plant a grain of wheat; watch it grow. Along with this activity read every child's favorite, *Little Red Hen,* a nursery tale adaptation. Show him flour and explain that it comes from wheat. Let him mix flour to help make bread or a cake. Ask him ways the family uses bread.

Cut two pieces of wax paper about 8x8. Have your child pick a green leaf from a tree. Place the leaf between the two pieces of wax paper. Put a towel over it. With a hot iron, press the wax paper together. Hang the picture up. In the fall, follow the same procedure with a leaf from the same tree and hang it by the other leaf. Read together what caused the change of color in the two leaves.

Seed catalogs give large brilliant pictures of flowers, trees, vegetables, and fruit. Go through a magazine together, naming the items. Sometimes it is difficult for a child to distinguish between cabbage and lettuce, oranges and tangerines, peaches and apples. If you have any of these foods, let him touch and taste them while you repeat the names to him. He may also observe the differences in foods at the grocery store.

There are intellectual qualities in rocks, animals, plants, and shells. Darla's children found some small logs cut down by beavers. They placed them among the shrubs and flowers in an attractive arrangement. Various rock formations give children interesting information. Many wild flowers are unique in color and shape. Encourage your child to transplant some to his own yard.

Tempt him with a surprise box on a rainy day, or on one of those "there's nothing to do" days. Supply the box with watercolors, finger paints, story books, rhythm band instruments (Many books tell how these can be made inexpensively) scissors, string, glue, construction paper, and bright scraps of fabric. His imagination will take over from there.

A traveling situation can be a learning time when

you are going from one place to another. Talk to him about vacation plans. Purchase a scrapbook and an inexpensive camera. Have him take pictures of scenes he wants. After the trip is over and the pictures have been developed, place the pictures in sequence and ask him what he would like you to write under each one.

Long trips can be tiring, specially to an active child. Every one hundred miles present him with a small surprise—a book, magnetic car game, "all day" sucker, activity book, puzzle, or the ever faithful coloring book and crayons. Vary the surprise. If you are familiar with the areas you are traveling, tell him to look for familiar scenes: a wheat field, oil well, snow on mountains, cactus, a bridge, or a river. When he spots what you have mentioned, praise him warmly; or perhaps even give him a gift.

There are many items convenient to make in the car to produce physical and mental activity. Make a whirling button. Pass a piece of string through two holes of a large button. Tie the ends of the string together. Making sure the button is in the middle, hold the ends of the string with both hands and swing the button around and around. As the button makes a circle, it will twist the string. Pull on the ends of the string. The string will unwind and whirl the button so fast it will wind the string in the opposite direction. Keep pulling, then let the string twist.

Create a scratch painting. Color a piece of heavy white paper with a crayon. Using an object such as a hairpin for your tool, scratch away parts of the crayon to make the desired picture.

Blow up balloons, making sure they stay away from the driver. Use a magic marker to make faces, scenes, or abstract designs.

Art can be a delightful form of mental expression in the home. At this age the only learning involved in painting is not to drip the paint and not to scrub through the paper. The child has one goal, sheer joy in color and activity. He will not have a preplanned picture; that will come later. Give him freedom in this activity, for it may become the basic foundation for his formal teaching. In any activity, independence is what you are always building toward.

Give all art work a place of honor. Joan sets a tall easel in her living room to display Keith's kindergarten art portfolio. Visitors comment on his work and encourage him to continue doing well with it.

Cardboard egg cartons can be used to make paper tulips. Cut out each egg holder; then paint each one with a different watercolor. Put a green pipe cleaner through the bottom for a stem and make green construction paper leaves. Glue these to the stem. Put a small piece of clay in the bottom of a small vase or basket and stick the stems in it. If it is the right time of year, help him plant tulip bulbs and study about the care of them. You may want to add to this learning process by reading books about Holland. Introduce your child to the story of *Hans Brinker and the Silver Skates* by Mary Mapes Dodge.

Help your child learn colors a fascinating way. Use broken egg shells carefully washed and dried. Fix different colors of Easter egg dye. Drop the broken egg shells into the dye. Remove, dry and crumble and shells onto different pieces of newspaper, keeping the colors separated. As you work, talk together about the names of the colors. Construct a simple penciled landscape on poster paper. Spread glue lightly where the grass will be, and sprinkle the green shells on it. Follow the same procedure for trees, water, sky, and sun. Make all the objects large because your preschooler is not ready for small detailed pictures. After the art work has dried, hang it and point to the various colors, asking him to name them.

Have him color one side of a 3x5 card the color of each crayon in his basic set of colored crayons. Flash this card to him and have him tell you the color. This not only teaches him color but also introduces him to the flash cards he will meet when he starts to school.

Music creates different moods for different children. Choose choice records that produce vivid mental pictures to the listener. This challenges mental growth. Some records give directions for your child to follow (you can follow with him).

Select records with simple rhythms. Make rhythm band instruments. The bottom of a wastecan becomes a drum. Sandpaper nailed to small wooden blocks makes a scraping sound. Two wooden dowels are rhythm sticks. Buy jingle bell rings. You may want to use your hands to beat out rhythms on a hard surface.

Purchase records that give the sounds of stringed, brass, woodwind, and percussion instruments. Listen to classical, western, and pop music, and various ensembles. Soon your child will detect the names of the instruments and the types of music being played.

Most children enjoy pets. How fortunate a child is to have a mom who doesn't mind (too much) stepping on spilled hamster seed, who helps nurture a crippled baby bird, housebreak a pup, or bury a pet, and cries with her child as he learns about death. You may think you could never handle a white mouse or a rabbit, but you can because you can see how interested your child is in this aspect of life. Let him feed and observe different characteristics that appear over a period of weeks. These visual aids teach valuable lessons.

When Dana was five years old, her dad secured a gentle horse for her during the summer months. They built a makeshift fence. Dana had the responsibility of feeding, watering, brushing, and exercising her horse. She was proud of her efforts when it was time for her birthday and she was able to let each of her guests ride.

Mom, spend these first years prodding your child's curiosities. It will help him succeed in his formal education.

# ELEMENTARY

How long has it been since you have lain on your stomach and watched ants store food for winter? When did you look closely at the construction of a bird's nest? How long has it been since you watched a squirrel dig for hidden nuts? Can you remember running through rows of tall corn or marveling at a field of wild daisies or tasting warm milk from a cow? You experienced many of life's simple pleasures while growing up, and now it is your child's turn.

He will be full of questions. He will need time to be alone; time to be with his family. He will need large amounts of uninterrupted time to do meaningful activities. Encourage him to go into new situations. Rehearse with him what to say and how to handle himself in new and strange surroundings.

He is now reaching a turning point in his mental development. He will begin thinking to reach conclusions. Up until now you have been "the authority" on every question asked. And now—"But mom, my teacher said. . . ." The teacher will have much influence on your child, but you will continue to have time to arouse his curiosity in other areas and expand on the knowledge he receives at school.

His success at school will be determined by the educational qualities you provide in the home. Help your child to think highly of himself. Compliment, praise, and encourage him for any accomplishment. When he experiences success in his home, is allowed to participate in daily activities, and is treated with respect and courtesy, he cannot help meeting new situations with success.

You are motivating him when he succeeds in a given task. Include him in talks about some of the family problems; let him help work out vacation plans. When his ideas are accepted, he will want to learn more in order to contribute more. Help him experience success with a problem he can handle.

Everytime he succeeds, it will intensify his desire to learn more, to think, and to create.

Your first grader will be eager to learn. His new adjustments will depend on how well you have prepared him beforehand. If you will be aware of the new procedures facing him, you can work with him before school begins. Help him get acquainted with the physical structure of the school building. Tell him about his teacher. Explain that he will be in a large group and will learn how to fit into the group effectively. Explain some of the rules he may have concerning bathroom privileges, as well as classroom, lunchroom, and playground rules.

In his first year he will learn to listen, recite, read, and write. This is indeed an important year. If you detect a problem that may be affecting his learning, call the school and make an appointment to counsel with his teacher to see if the problem can be solved. Many teachers are unaware that personal problems exist.

Give your young student a good send-off each morning. This statement sounds simple; but running a smooth household before the school day begins demands effort on your part. Give him a warm greeting when he comes home from school. Sit down and listen to his day's activities. If you can help him meet the new demands of school at this age, he will be successful as an adolescent when greater demands are made.

Because your child's ability to concentrate and conceive new ideas is highly developed between the ages of six and thirteen, remain alert during this time to help him look, listen, and search for knowledge.

Take time to attend his school functions. Become an active P.T.A. member; volunteer for school activities; become acquainted with his teachers. All of this indicates how much you value your child's school.

Occasionally some children do not like school. If

this happens, talk with him and encourage him to express his dislikes. Talk with his teacher or school counselor. There may be a physical problem with seeing or hearing. He may be embarrassed about using the restroom. *The Boy Who Would Not Go to School,* by Munro Leaf, could help solve some of your child's problems. Mr. Leaf shows through simple language and pictures the fun children miss by not going to school.

Your child may need help with his homework. If he is having trouble in a certain area, provide a quiet atmosphere and remain calm when you are unable to help him. In beginning math, you might use interesting objects to help him comprehend addition and subtraction. Use popcorn, dried beans, fruit, sticks, or even canned goods.

When Pamela had completed her first reading primer and was allowed to bring it home, she lined up her family on the divan, pulled up her chair to face the group and read with as much expression as she could the story of *Run, Dick, Run.* The family applauded. This was her proud moment. Her teacher had introduced her to a new look in the world of knowledge and she had succeeded.

Donna observed the new words her daughters were learning in school. She set up a large easel and chalk board in the living room and each morning printed a message to greet the girls. It was never a problem getting them out of bed because they were so eager to translate the daily messages.

Ray was very patriotic during the first and second grade. He learned the names of all the presidents, their terms, and many outstanding accomplishments of some of them. His mother took him to the public library often and helped him look for material. She read many of the presidents' biographies to him and purchased a set of books on the subject. He made frequent trips to a book store and searched through any available books. At one point his parents told him they could not buy him any more books. He had also exhausted his accumulated allowance. In the meantime he found a book he felt he had to have. In desperation he sold his bike in order to purchase the book. (He had already asked for a new bike for Christmas.) His request for new spring clothes that year was "red, white, and blue." Betty bought him white pants, a navy jacket, a white shirt, and a red tie. Some family friends gave him an American flag which he anchored to the front of the house to fly every day. In his room he was allowed to hang news clippings and posters which pertained to anything patriotic. Later he was privileged to go to Washington, D.C., to see the historic sights. His mom took time to encourage and honor his requests. Ray's interest included some financial backing, but there was also a tremendous amount of time on the part of his mother to grant to him the knowledge he was looking for.

Beverly had a "stroke of genius" one summer. Circumstances caused her and her children to spend six weeks with her mother. Her mother was elderly and usually rested each afternoon. "How can I keep the children quiet while mother rests?" Beverly talked with the children about the idea of having school in the afternoon from 1:00-3:00. The children liked the idea and they began making plans immediately. Mom became "Miss Momma." The children had an altogether different attitude toward her while she was their teacher.

Their schedule not only included the three R's, but also physical education, art, music, and home living. Alice needed help in English so she read various books, had memory work, and learned to make proper book reports. Robert was kindergarten age. He had subjects in reading readiness and elementary math. For physical education they followed the program published by the President's Council on Physical Fitness. It was a very rigorous program. Mom also participated.

For her home living course, Beverly demonstrated how to clean a sink, how to sweep and dust properly, and how to do other forms of housework. The children became personally responsible for certain chores later. In personal grooming, Robert knew he could not leave for "school" until his hair was combed. He did it readily and with no coaxing.

Report cards were given out when school was over. The children made out invitations for commencement and mailed them to their neighborhood friends. During the program the children shared what they had learned during summer school.

All of this took time, but to a mother and her children it was a total success. You may not be able to present a teaching program such as this to your child, but you may take portions of it and form some similar learning situations during those long summer months.

There is great value in parents and children doing things together. It is the only way parents can impart ideals to their children. The average child usually spends a large amount of time with his teacher, school activities, and friends. The family has what little time is left to be a strong influence, and therefore must value the time spent as a family unit for learning times together.

Suggest starting an insect zoo for a summer project. Place a large table in the garage. Let your child decide what his collection will include. By observing a caterpillar spinning his cocoon, your child will be eager to see what emerges. Help him catch butterflies, learning to identify and mount them. Make a trip to the park to find various insect species. An ant farm is an inexpensive item that can be purchased through a mail order service. Have your child keep a log book and register daily changes in his insects.

You may know someone personally who has a farm. Choose a day when no one is rushed for time and enjoy the country together. Allow your child to feed some of the animals, hold a piglet, pet a lamb, ride a horse, milk a cow, gather eggs, and study the habits of each animal. If your timing is right, allow him to watch the birth of an animal. Imagine the memories your child would have from a day like this!

Finding a turtle is not an ordinary discovery. Let your child observe one for several days, watch his eating habits, see how he protects himself, and study his structure. Before you give the turtle his freedom, print your child's name and address on the shell. If the turtle is found by someone else, your child may receive a letter from the next young owner.

Give your child gifts that challenge his imagination. Let him observe a chicken incubator and watch the chicks being hatched. You can purchase small plastic scale models for the study of human anatomy. If he has acquired an interest in inventing, obtain an elementary chemistry set. With each gift you will want to encourage him to read, observe, care for, and invent on his level of learning.

The elementary years are "collecting" years. Rocks are favorite items. If you are planning a vacation to several states, suggest he find rock samples from the different states, identify them, and compare them with the other rocks. Boys, in particular, might find arrowhead-hunting fascinating. Watch for freshly plowed fields close to a creek or river. These will be your best areas. With this activity, provide authentic Indian stories for him to read. Find pictures at the public library on how the different sized and shaped arrowheads were used. Make or buy him an Indian suit, complete with moccasins. If interest is high enough, plan a vacation to include a visit to an Indian Reservation. Give him a chance to see Indian pottery, basket weaving, and rug making.

Coin and stamp collecting, a leaf study, mushroom hunting, a wild flower collection—all of these activities require a certain amount of research. Go "junkin'." Visit antique stores. Study periods of furniture and objects that are unfamiliar to your child. Be ready to take time with your child if he shows unusual interest in any of these areas.

Get permission to visit a fire station, dairy, cheese factory, saw mill, hosiery mill, the city water department, police station, or to tour historical homes. See what could be made available to you in your community. Follow through with family discussions or book study.

Many families live in a mobile world. You may find it effective in helping your child make his new environmental adjustments by visiting points of interest while waiting to get better acquainted with other children. This creates good mental calisthenics.

Help your child to develop an appreciation for the fine arts. Check your newspaper or call the Chamber of Commerce to see what is available in your community. Take opportunities to attend public organ, piano, or vocal concerts, orchestras, and choirs. Take tours of art museums. Many cities have Little Theatre drama productions.

The Brooks family created a different Christmas exchange that called for the use of some mental faculties. For weeks Alice and her mother practiced a piano duet composition of Bach's "Jesu, Joy of Man's Desiring." This was Alice's gift to her dad. The children were taken ice skating and to a stage production for their gifts. The oldest child was taken to see *The Nutcracker Suite* ballet before the holidays. For her grandparents, Alice wrote and illustrated poems and bound them in book form for their gift. You may want to build on this idea by including your child's original written stories and art work, along with photographs of the young author.

By the age of six or seven your child should begin having a fairly good concept of words and numbers. A Scrabble game should encourage him to create new words. He will work harder when he is competing. Each day at the meal table, present a new word from the dictionary to your family. Every member is to use the word in a sentence to another family member before the day is over. Use words that will benefit him in expressing himself effectively.

Many mothers are realizing the game of Monopoly is highly educational, specially teaching the number concept. At five years of age, Bob learned to make change and handle his own money with this game. Although he could not look ahead and plan his strategy, he did have a good concept of dealing with numbers. Jacks and dominoes are also useful in presenting numbers to your child.

In the later elementary years you will notice if your child is developing special interests. If art is his specialty, provide adequate art supplies. You may check into the possibilities of having him take private art lessons. He may show a strong interest in the piano. Be careful in your selection of a teacher from the beginning. She should have a genuine love for, interest in, and understanding of children, besides being sound in theory and ready to provide a variety of music. Sing with your child, play duets with him, and on occasion sit with him as he practices. These are excellent activities to help him release unhealthy emotions in a socially accepted way.

Books are magic. They can make a sick child feel better; a sad child, happy; a restless child, calm; a disagreeable child, cooperative.

Listen as your child reads to you. Have him practice telling a story, record his selection, and keep a continuous tape for him to enjoy.

Let him see a book being made by taking time to visit a printing press. Provide room areas for him to shelve his books properly. He may want to prepare his own simple card catalog system. Present him a book subscription for birthdays and other special events. Have his favorite frayed books rebound as special gifts. It may take some readjusting of the family budget, but this is definitely the time to purchase that set of encyclopedias. It is an indispensable teaching aid for any home.

Through these years your child will be learning how to live successfully with others, and how to overcome problems. Many libraries have the book *Behavior Patterns in Children's Books* compiled by Clara J. Kircher. This book lists the authors and the names of children's books that present various teaching situations. Examples of some of the sections are: "Consideration for Others," "Cooperation," "Friendship," "Growing Up," "Helpfulness," "Acceptance of a New Baby," "Family Relations," "Appreciation of Others," "Obedience," "Courage," and "Generosity." Under each section available books are listed. Almost any lesson you are trying to get your child to learn can be found in this book.

Activity books can give him hours of pleasure. See what he will do with these books by Vernon Howard: *Here's Fun with Riddles; Things a Boy Can Do; Things a Girl Can Do; 500 Games for Boys and Girls; Laugh Awhile Skits and Stunts 1, 2, 3;* and *Easy Handcrafts for Juniors.*

Richard Scarry's book *What Do People Do All Day?* will help your child create his own plans for the day. The Weekly Reader Book Club produces well-written books for children. Your child's school can provide the address. Take him to the library and teach him how to choose his own books.

Beverly summarized the feelings of many mothers about the importance of mental development for children. "Some may say I have not fulfilled myself by doing so many things with my children, but I do feel it is important to give them the right start. I definitely feel a mother should give her time freely, willingly, and happily with her children."

## HIGH SCHOOL

Before this age level you have involved yourself with your child. You have helped him to see that he is a unique individual, capable of responding success-fully in tasks that have been presented to him.

Many of the ideas you have introduced in the past now become specialized in certain areas. He now begins to reason and think logically. He will begin to consider future plans for himself and include his desires to help society. He will start the awkward process of emancipating himself from his parents by choosing a satisfying career. You will experience mixed emotions about your child's becoming independent of your care and your ideas, but we must all let go when the time is right. By now you will have developed a mutual respect for each other. You will want to uphold him in the decisions he must make for his future.

It is highly beneficial for parents to understand this stage of growth. In the book *Nursing Care of Children*, by Blake, Wright, and Waechter, there is a section relating to the intellectual development of the adolescent. The goal of the adolescent is presented: how he functions intellectually, how he faces paren-tal problems, how he reaches maturity, and how he must participate in extracurricular activities for emo-tional outlets (pp. 522-37).

He will be confronted with problems and stress, but he will learn from these experiences. Although it is hard for you to watch him work through these events, try to keep in mind that he will be a stronger and wiser individual when he succeeds in working through his problems. You will be there to help him gain a strong, flexible ego. Suggest that he keep a daily journal. This is to be a private endeavor of writing out his hopes, questions, and dreams. This will help him build a good self-concept. A wise man once said, "Know thyself." Encourage your child to do just that.

The school curriculum will offer opportunities to help him see what fields are most challenging. Talk with him about including courses in his schedule that may indicate a latent aptitude in a particular area.

If your child shows interest in the medical profession, he may not only want to take as many science classes as possible but he may want to work in a hospital—either as a salaried worker or as a volunteer. Have him discuss his interest with the family doctor. If the doctor feels he is seriously considering the medical field, he might arrange to show your teen the possible areas of work.

Journalism may interest him. The school newspaper or yearbook could give him added experience. Working in a newspaper office might also be beneficial.

Art can be developed by helping with scenery for stage productions and parade floats or by joining an active art club. Many teen-agers are making a profitable business during their high school years by designing original art ideas and selling them privately or through gift shops.

Dana asked her dad to saw a small tree limb into ¼ inch thicknesses. She sanded and sealed each disc, painted the school emblem on one side and the name of the school on the other, finished them with a coat of varnish, drilled a small hole in them, and sold them as key chains for both experienced and potential young drivers.

Pam made elaborate rings from Play-Doh, shaping them and letting them dry thoroughly. She painted bright designs on them with a glossy lacquer paint. The result: standing orders from her classmates.

Give your consent to let your teen-ager create his own room atmosphere. The color scheme might be different from what you would plan; but, most importantly, it will satisfy him. Work with him in making a ceiling-to-floor bulletin board covered with burlap, or have the bulletin board extend across the bottom half of one wall. This will make his displayed memories eye level when he is lying on his bed daydreaming.

He can have picture groupings on his wall with

various plaques made from scrap lumber. The design for the board can be made from poster board. Paint the design with airplane paint, glue it to the board, let it dry, and finally antique the entire surface.

Teen-agers enjoy candles for a personal room atmosphere. They can make different shapes using egg or milk cartons, plastic containers, or they can make small thin candles to float in a bowl of water.

A rug for his room does not have to be expensive. Suggest going to furniture stores and securing small rug scraps. Many stores throw their scraps away. Help work out a design. Cut the different shapes with a hook knife. Join the pieces with rug stripping tape or get the backing that large rugs come packed in, glue the rug pieces to the burlap side of the backing with a strong adhesive glue, and so create an original design.

Make wall shelves from old boards and brackets. Pam found a wooden cold air grate, painted it black and attached light-weight black chains to the front ends, then hung it on the wall. It made a serviceable, attractive shelf for her bedroom.

Many young people are becoming aware of the possibilities of working in summer camps as counselors, secretaries, receptionists, or maintenance workers. This is an excellent opportunity for him to experience the growing desire of being independent. He will have complete responsibility of his living quarters, his physical well-being, living on a budget, as well as taking full responsibility for working successfully under all types of circumstances. He will experience what it is like to live in the organized work world and to be completely responsible for his behavior. This experience could show him if he enjoys organizing and working with others or if he should eliminate this possibility and realize that he works more effectively alone.

Good baby-sitters are always in demand. From the time he begins this activity, provide him with some good books to help him understand the ages he will be working with. A job he may think to be simple really is a good learning experience. This could lead to a vocation that deals with children, such as teaching or counseling.

An interest in sewing could branch out into specialized fields of fashion design, interior design, merchandising, store management, and other commercialized possibilities.

Do you have a son who enjoys working on old cars? It may seem like so much dirt, grease, and grimy laundry to you, mom, but this may be an early beginning of his interest in the field of mechanics. Bear with him—he's searching. Many youths of this age are choosing what truly interests them, instead of jobs that are known for their social prestige. His satisfaction with what he produces is the most important aspect for his chosen vocation.

During his junior year of high school you will want to start discussing with him the possibilities of higher education. Take different days off to visit educational facilities. Do not be alarmed if he doesn't choose your alma mater—or any college. The final decision must be his, and you are wise to let him make that final decision.

From birth you have asked God how you could help your child find his life's purpose. He has been taught by you the glorious worth of God's creation, and now his vocational choice will help him make his world a better world.

Through the years you have not had time to wonder why you have gone to so many recitals, band concerts, parades, sports events, joined P.T.A., helped make election posters, made trips to the library, helped with homework, or found new ways to get paint off a rug or grease from clothes. William Cowper said, "God works in mysterious ways His wonders to perform." Now the greatest gift you can offer this important individual in your life is to help him accept these two promises from God's Word: "As thou goest step by step I will open up the way before thee" (Prov. 4:12 Syr.); and "Call unto me and I will answer you and show you great and mighty things, fenced in and hidden, which you do not know—do not distinguish and recognize, have knowledge of and understand" (Jer. 33:3 Amp.).

# Take Time to Develop

## "stature"

Hanging in our bedroom is a faded sheet of construction paper with the outline of two tiny hands and the picture of a small girl. By the picture is this poem:

> *These are my hands*
> *So tiny, so small*
> *To hang somewhere*
> *Upon the wall,*
> *For us to see*
> *As the years roll by*
> *How fast we grow*
> *My hands and I.*
>
> –Unknown

Look into those puffy, unobservant eyes of your baby. He seems to have too much skin for his body. There is no definite chin line, no visible signs of coordination; but he is one of the most beautiful creations your eyes have ever seen. This thought occurs to you, "How will I ever be able to help this precious child in his physical development?" How important is this stage of life? "Haven't you yet learned that your body is the home of the Holy Spirit God gave you, and that He lives within you? Your own body does not belong to you. For God has bought you with a great price. So use every part of your body to give glory back to God, because He owns it" (I Cor. 6:19-20 TLB). Now you have your answer. This area of life is as sacred as the spiritual training you will want to give your child. A strong body is an asset to everyone. Take time in developing it.

# INFANCY

The warm milk you provide is your baby's first taste of nourishment. Within a matter of weeks he will graduate to solid foods. The patient way you introduce cereal into that unsuspecting mouth may prove to be the beginning of enjoyment for other new tastes. Offer the food in a spoon (a demitasse spoon is an excellent size) pressing the spoon lightly into the upper part of the mouth. This process makes it easier for your baby to take the food. That is quite a step for one so small. In fact, it's almost considered hard work by a baby's standard. Small portions to begin with are readily accepted and, because you took time and did not rush this new procedure, your baby has an excellent commencement in his physical growth.

How do you tolerate a baby with mashed potatoes in his hair, his clothing soiled for the third time that day, and his tray smeared beyond recognition? Be realistic. Your baby, now turned toddler, will want to feed himself. When he begins turning his head, clamping his mouth tightly shut and grabbing for the spoon, this is your clue. If you do not relish the thought of mopping the floor after each meal, place papers around the high chair and throw them away after the meal. It is an admirable way to recycle paper!

If the tray on which your toddler eats is constructed in such a way as to hold the food, place bits of each food in easy reach. He will need time to do some research. To introduce a new vegetable, place one green bean, a bite size of carrot, or whatever vegetable you are serving, on his tray. If he accepts it, add more. By careful observation you begin to detect the toddler's likes and dislikes. You will not become an over-anxious mother if you keep in mind that most toddlers will have a declining appetite at this age. When he approaches his third year, he will begin imitating his parents' eating habits by eating well-rounded meals.

The home extension department in any city gives free literature on the basic four foods for tasty, balanced, attractive meals: meat, fruit and vegetables, dairy products, bread and cereals. This department also has pamphlets showing various ways to prepare these foods. Mom, take time to read this type of information. It will help you create a healthier family.

Just as important as the food you furnish is the equipment you have ready for muscle development. Take time to read what should be made available at the appropriate age so you will not get ahead of your child's development.

In his eyesight development he may enjoy staring at his mom. He may stare intently at moving curtains. Mobiles will fascinate him for hours. He needs much visual stimulation. Place brightly colored pictures around the crib, possibly created by the older children. You will see those eyes begin to focus on the colors. Can you sense the importance expressed by the young artists who made those pictures?

# PRESCHOOL

Mealtime with a preschooler can be dreaded or challenging, hectic or relaxing. His appetite is on the decline, but here your ingenuity takes over.

To begin with, it may be necessary to buy a more expensive brand of food which has a milder taste. Keep in mind to go for quality until a particular food has been accepted.

Did you ever think of making up names for foods?

Mashed potatoes become "mountains", broccoli and green beans, "trees"; grapes, "balls"; gravy in the center of mashed potatoes, "swimming pools"; the yolk of the eggs, "the sun." By this age your child is becoming acquainted with others outside your home. Because cooked cereals are not eye appealing but rich in nutrition, let each spoonful eaten represent the name of a person he knows. When you begin going through names in each family, the bowl becomes empty, nourishment has been taken, and your child has vivid mental pictures of those who are entering his world.

Is it necessary for you always to be cooking and seasoning foods? You may discover that raw vegetables are sometimes more popular. A relish plate of raw carrots, celery, radishes, and cauliflower could provide the essential vegetables he needs. Keep these items cleaned and placed in a plastic bag so your child can have access to them between meals. He cannot ruin his appetite for the next meal with this type of snack. Raw fruit could be served in the same manner.

A protein-filled recipe, sure to be a favorite of any preschooler is:

### Finger Gelatin

Three 3-oz. packages red gelatin (any flavor)
3 cups boiling water
4 envelopes unflavored gelatin
1 cup cold water
2 tablespoons lemon juice

*Dissolve red gelatin in boiling water. Soften unflavored gelatin in the cold water. Add the red gel mixture and stir until dissolved. Add lemon juice and stir. Pour into a flat cake pan. Chill until firm. Cut into squares. Will not melt. Will not stick.*

This recipe can be placed on the kitchen counter through the day or be set on a low shelf in the refrigerator where your child can pick it up easily with his fingers. You whet his appetite for sweets and you can be assured he is receiving right nutrition —voluntarily.

Quite often a preschooler has not acquired a taste for dairy products. Some morning why don't you take time with him to make butter? You will need a small box of whipping cream, salt, a mixing bowl, spoon, and mixer.

*Whip cream until butter globules cling together. Use a spoon to press out remaining liquid and pour off. Rinse the butter with cold water. Add a pinch of salt and mix thoroughly. Form into a ball and place on a saucer.*

Have an impromptu morning break of a glass of milk and hot buttered toast. He will enjoy the taste because he helped make it.

Attractive fruit salads can enhance the table and can be made to look so delectable that no prompting is required to make them disappear.

### Raggedy Ann Salad

*Place a peach half upside down on a lettuce leaf. Use raisins for eyes and nose, a strip of pimiento for the mouth. Use finely shredded carrots for the hair, held securely by a thin amount of mayonnaise or softened cream cheese.*

### Grape Cluster Surprise Salad

*Place one 3-ounce package of cream cheese in bowl. Mix with two tablespoons of milk. Wash grapes, cut in half, remove seeds. Place one-half of a canned pear upside down on a lettuce leaf; spread cream cheese over pear. Arrange grape halves all over pear.*

### Peter Rabbit Salad

*Place one-half pear upside down on lettuce leaf. Use marshmallow quarters for ears, half for tail. Nose is a cherry bit, eyes are cloves.*

With these salads you have initiated three fascinating

fruit dishes. You could have simply cut up the fruit and served it in a bowl. You knew it would take more time to be inventive, but the important thing is that you created a desire for your child to see that eating can be fun.

Developing touch, taste, and smell, combined with mystery, wakes up the imagination with any child, specially when he is served a "Surprise Cup." The cup might contain small bits of apple, miniature marshmallows, seedless grapes, raisins, cookies, bananas, peanuts, or dry cereal. Either blindfold your child or have him sit in a darkened room. Place the cup in his hand. Let him feel each item, smell it, taste it, and guess what it is. He will be eating foods he might normally reject.

Health habits are conducive to better physical development. Many mothers have mentioned the problems that erupt during "hairwashing time." Margaret says, "You can call it bribery but my method worked!" She had always dreaded washing her preschooler's hair because the child cried from the first mention of the word until the ordeal was over. A beautician gave Margaret this idea. When the crying begins, quietly say, "Listen, do you hear a blue jay? You must be quiet or you can't hear him." Continue by saying, "Sometimes a blue jay will leave a small surprise after your hair is washed." Because a child enjoys repetition, you could add to the story or merely keep telling him to "listen." Soon the dreaded experience is over and a treat is given. This could range from a piece of candy to an occasional small picture book, ice cream cone, cookies, sugarless gum, and so on.

Make sure your child is in a comfortable position before the procedure begins. He may want to hold a towel to wipe any water that might get on his face. Telling make-up stories or sharing experiences you had as a child are fascinating attention-getters. It is delightful to see how he actually begins to look forward to having his hair washed. None of these extra activities last forever, but it does help your child overcome known fears in an acceptable way.

Bath time seldom creates a problem. Most youngsters relish the thought of being in water. Just so it can be kept appealing, provide bubbles (a mild dish-washing soap is good) and plastic cups to fill to make "ice cream sodas." The filling of the cups actually helps develop the use of smaller muscles. A soft sponge mit to fit your child's hand helps him bathe himself. Using soap shaped as animals or fruit also adds to the fun.

Play equipment for this age should be simple. Your preschooler will need a place to run, climb, and dig. Blessed is the mom who can ignore a cluttered house and bald spots in the lawn.

At the twelfth month your child will become accurate in placing objects where desired. You may notice him putting a lid on a pan. Why not provide three-piece wooden puzzles and educational toys that emphasize putting different-shaped objects into certain openings?

Get a sandbox ready for warm weather. Have old spoons, plastic containers, pails, shovels, small cars, or anything to create the mood for play while he develops muscle skills. A trip to a near-by park where play equipment is available can help absorb boundless energy.

One summer we had just finished painting the exterior of our house. Our toddler showed interest in the procedure, but she knew she could not help in the effort. She was content to play close by with her toys. After our job was finished, we provided her with a small pail of water and a three inch paint brush, and she "painted" the house hour after hour. Until recently she thought she had actually helped paint the house. This activity helped her use her arm muscles and at the same time provided entertainment.

When your child is two, secure a board about ten or

twelve inches wide and several feet long. Set it on low blocks and work with your child in developing balance. He will want to experiment with walking up and down steps, swinging on low bars, crawling in, out, on top, and around packing boxes and banging on peg boards.

When the third year comes around, small muscles begin to function *if* you take time to provide the proper tools. If you stay alert and dare to give him a pair of blunt scissors, he will cut incessantly. *Remember*: always give him something appropriate to cut. He may find it equally exciting to cut his hair, your curtains, or sashes off dresses. Offer him old catalogs and bright construction paper. Glue the cut-out pictures on the construction paper. Edith began this practice when the family made trips to see the grandparents. It made the trip go much quicker. Pushing cinnamon sticks into styrofoam balls requires a certain amount of muscle coordination. With that job done, the ball can be hung on a bright string and hung in the kitchen to enhance your decor!

Continue to help him along by encouraging water painting with large paint brushes or by hammering nails in old pieces of lumber, and by purchasing a blackboard, complete with colored chalk. It is a good idea to place a newspaper under the blackboard to catch the chalk dust.

Preschoolers have their expected times of chicken pox, mumps, measles, and colds. You know how vital liquids are for treatment in many of these illnesses. Be one step ahead of your child. Instead of saying, "The doctor said you must drink lots of water." or "If you will drink liquids you will get better faster," get original. Every boy or girl should have in his possession a toy tea set. Wash it thoroughly. In the small pitcher add at various times throughout the day, warm tea, juices, or water. Sure, your house needs attention, you are behind in all your work because of one small patient, but in the midst of it all take time for a "party." Before the end of the day, sufficient liquid has been consumed and it has been one more pleasant experience for patient and mom.

Invest in a "sick" glass. It is a plastic glass which has a built-in straw on the side. It can be purchased at almost any grocery, drug, or variety store. Use it ONLY when your child is ill. It becomes a special item and another way to encourage liquid intakes.

Not only medicine and liquids, but extra rest is a necessity during an illness. Quiet games, reading aloud, or making simple crafts will fulfill the needs of a fretful child. Taking time to go to the public library for ideas could be beneficial. Grocery stores carry a number of activity books for any age. A new coloring book and a small box of crayons never become commonplace. Sitting by your child, color one page and have him color the opposite page. Help him put his initials and the date on his work. This will help him remember "a day with mom" when he gets in school and learns to read.

Toilet training is essential to good physical development. How many mothers have dreaded this time in their preschooler's life? Realize from the first that just because your friend's child has begun with success does not necessarily mean your child is ready. Between the fifteenth and eighteenth month begin checking your clock at two-hour intervals to see if your child can retain urine for this length of time. If so, this could be the time to being toilet training for urination.

A toilet chair is good because he can use it himself. Have a good supply of training pants from the beginning. It will be important for him to experience that good sensation of being dry. It will be an aggravation when his only pair of shoes gets wet, but keep a pair of inexpensive house shoes on hand for him to wear while you are drying his good ones. A warm oven could speed this process, or you can place the wet shoes close to a heat register.

Before you set your child on his toilet chair, put a small amount of warm water into the pot. If this is not effective, let him hear running water from the sink. Some toilet chairs have trays. If at first your child seems to detest this new experience of training, place a small book or a favorite toy on the tray, sit by him and either read or make up a story about the toy. Save special play articles for this time. Every time will not be successful; but take time to praise him, if only for sitting on his chair. Would you believe he enjoys seeing and hearing your pleasure over his accomplishment?

The most effective times to place him on his toilet chair might be before bedtime, first thing each morning, after a nap, and after meals. Limiting his liquid intake before bedtime may help him succeed in staying dry throughout the night. Some mothers who have been successful in keeping their child dry in the daytime but not at night have tried placing their child on his chair at 10:00 P.M. Speak softly to your child and encourage him to urinate. On the other hand, if he finds it hard to get back to sleep, this may not be the time to start this stage of training.

It is customary to say that by three and one-half to four and one-half years of age, elimination is in control. Some children are highly successful in a shorter length of time; others are not. Try hard to concentrate on not comparing children; it will only frustrate you. As long as you are taking time, being patient and relaxed in face of accidents, you will help that pre-schooler succeed.

During all these phases of physical development, activity, and training, you have become a diligent observer. Look at your child, watch him run, listen to all the noise he makes. See his eyes sparkle when you suggest another intriguing activity. Before you are fully aware of all the time you have spent together "in sickness and in health," you have helped him graduate into the elementary years. He is anxious, but is ready, because you took time to help him develop for this moment.

# ELEMENTARY

There is so much excitement on the very first day of school that your first grader may not feel like eating. Fix a pretty table with a fresh flower at each plate, plus a centerpiece made of a box of crayons, pencils, chalk, small books covers made of construction paper—anything depicting school. Greet him at the table with "Happy first year in school."

You may be tempted to shortchange your family by not cooking. So you're not a "morning" person. Discipline yourself to see the significance of this beginning hour with a school child. He will be a better student if a daily practice of eating breakfast is established. Think of all the available foods for breakfast; then make varied combinations of them. Ask occasionally what he would like to have. If the answer is "a hamburger"—great. It is full of protein and you have an all-American child living with you.

There is a strong possibility that vegetables are still not favorite foods. You do not live in a time when a garden is a necessity; but if a child helps grow a small vegetable garden, weed, hoe, water, and harvest it, there will be no doubt that he will enjoy the fruits from it. Let him help choose the seeds. Plant a short row of each. Add two or three tomato plants. A small garden plot takes little room and the self-satisfaction is most rewarding.

When your child is older, he may find pleasure in helping prepare a meal. Without a doubt he will eat any dish he helps prepare, even if it tastes repulsive. The fun in the preparation is heightened if mom doesn't assist too much. You may want to purchase a junior cookbook. Have him responsible for planning a menu from the book. See if the menu is well balanced. "Have you included the basic four?" This one simple rule will be passed on when he institutes his own home. Shop together, comparing quality and prices. Now the chef is ready to create.

A sixth grade boy's mother was asked out for lunch. Her son said, "Mom, you go on. I'll babysit and fix lunch for the kids. By the way, aren't we having company tonight? I'll bake the cake for you." The kids had a lunch of soup 'n' sandwiches, the cake was baked, and one mom had a well-deserved time out from her daily routine. The next day she bought her son a cookbook and put his name in it, "in appreciation." A verbal "thank you" would have been sufficient, but she took time to express her sentiment in a lasting and thoughtful way.

How do you introduce your family to casseroles effectively? If you can get your husband's absolute cooperation, the imitators will follow. This recipe could be the answer for a starter.

### "Sure Thing" Casserole

1½ pound hamburger, browned and drained

Place in a 2½ quart dish

Add one bag of egg noodles, 1 can of tomato soup, 1 can of cream of mushroom soup, 1 can of cheddar cheese soup.

Bake in 350° oven for one hour.

(This is even better warmed up.)

From this beginning you can concoct numerous hamburger casseroles. When you serve it on an attractively set table with hot bread and a "surprise" dessert, be ready to hear, "Mom, how can you make hamburger taste good so many ways?" "Sure was a good meal." "Kids, don't we have a good cook?"

A pleasant way to vary any mealtime is to serve it in different areas. How about breakfast outdoors on an early spring day, an evening meal by candlelight or kerosene lamps, or in the dining room on a snowy day if there is a wide view of the outdoors. An extra treat is a "once a week" meal in the family room on TV trays while you watch a family favorite show.

Mom, take time to create a period for play each day. Who wants to be remembered for always having clean closets and the ironing caught up? These are not top priority jobs with children.

You might be surprised how difficult it is for a six-year-old to bounce a ball. Purchase an inexpensive one and invent new ideas with it. Begin bouncing it back and forth to each other and see how far you can count before a miss. Throw it to each other, taking a step backward occasionally to see how far each of you can throw.

If you have several children in the neighborhood or you have invited some over for a special occasion, form relay lines, pass a ball over heads, through legs; pass it around in a circle like "hot potato." Relays are favorites. Run backward to a given point, hop, skip, duck walk, run sideways, bunny hop. Try bouncing a ball to a certain line and back. Competitive spirit keeps any game alive. Don't forget—you are a participiant, not just an organizer. Think of all the muscles you are using while creating activities for the younger set!

Take advantage of the seasons. During the onset of spring plan a family bike hike. Map out where you are going, pack an easy picnic lunch, and enjoy some glorious hours; travel at a pace where you can enjoy scenery as you never would in a car. A walking hike could be just as effective, besides giving one a chance to gather wild flowers, leaves, and rocks.

Many parents use summer for recreational time in developing their child's interests in sports. If you are fortunate to have skills in tennis, swimming, baseball, and other sports, you will do yourself a favor not only by teaching your child to enjoy these excellent opportunities but also by keeping yourself in shape. Lessons are available in many cities; it is a matter of finding which are worthwhile are taking advantage of them. As you may suspect, it could become a drudgery to take your child to swimming lessons each day. You've never had time to do needlework, read, catch up on correspondence? Here is the hour available for you. The young swimmer may never admit it, but he enjoys your being at his lessons to see his accomplishments. On the days when there are no lessons, go to the pool together and let him try his new knowledge on you. You can be the learner, him the teacher. It's good for his ego.

Being outdoors is a treat after a cold winter. Have jump ropes handy, join in a game of single or double hopscotch, go fishing. Salvage large cardboard refrigerator boxes for crawling in, out, and over. There are fewer restrictions and less adult supervision in this type of play, and such freedom is welcomed after nine months of organized school. Maybe you noticed through the school year that your child is not athletically inclined and has felt inferior during physical education classes. Take time during these summer months to practice chin ups, tumbling, batting balls, or whatever activity he needs practice in achieving. This might be all it takes to build up your child's confidence.

Provide a small plot for a flower garden. Let him take complete care of it. He will not only be nurturing his garden, but also nurturing his physical needs as well.

How long has it been since you have waded, skipped rocks, rowed a boat, saw how high you could swing, balanced a teeter totter, or climbed on bars? You may not last as long as your youngster, but seeing his mom "try" will bring laughter and memorable amusement as he tells dad "what my mom did today."

If you are fortunate to have a tall, sturdy tree in your yard, get your husband to throw a heavy rope over one of the larger branches. On the end place a stuffed burlap sack, tied securely to the rope. Sit on it to ensure safety and comfort. Have your child practice running and jumping on it and the aerial performance begins. Watch out your window at the smiles of the pilot soaring in his airplane and feeling the breeze on his face; and forget that one certain area of green grass has been short-lived.

Every tree house has its story. Every one you see shows that a mom or dad has helped stabilize a few planks in that tree to generate summer pleasure. For each step up to the house there are twenty nails securing it. For every nail there is a hammering session never to be excelled by any professional carpenter. These tree houses make good secret club meeting places or a spot for a child to sit and daydream on a lazy summer afternoon.

Most children have never made a leaf house in the fall. Equipment needed: a yard full of leaves, a rake for each builder and some crude household items. You may need to take time to help construct the first house, but after that a child's ingenuity takes possession. Decide how many rooms you will want. Begin raking in the area where you want the living room. Rake the leaves in lines of about twelve inches in height to form the shape of the room. Plan where the doorway will be and clear that space. Add the next room, and the next. The house begins to take shape. With construction completed, add empty cereal boxes, cans, milk cartons, and so on to the kitchen. Furnish the bedroom with a soft pile of leaves, with an old quilt or sheet for the leaf bed. In the living room pile leaves for divans and chairs.

Without thinking of all the clean-up value you have helped create, you have got your child into the fresh air, plus helping him use large and small muscles that are so essential to a healthy body. When he has completed playing in his house, you can suggest raking the same leaves into one large pile as a landing place for a jumping game.

Creativity comes from physical exercise, and a snowy day naturally means exercise. Oh, that the snowman never becomes extinct! Mom, don't lose your touch here. If the snow is wet and conducive to good snowman building, help your child make snowmen to represent each family member. It is fun to see which "member" lasts the longest. An older child may do some simple snow sculptures.

Sleigh riding is always a treat. Mom, get prepared. You will have clothes to dry all day. In many places it is permissible to build a fire where children are sledding. That warmth is looked forward to after he has fallen from his sled several times. Ed made his daughter a sled, painted it bright red, and painted her name on it. The result: a special sled, built for a child's special world.

What child would ever forget sleigh riding with his family at sunset? For the topping, ride to a cozy, warm house and a cup of hot chocolate. Here is a family favorite dry hot chocolate mix that is very quick to fix and easy to store:

### Dry Hot Chocolate Mix

*In a large mixing bowl*
*Mix:     8 quart box of dry milk powder*
*          6 ounce jar of non-dairy coffee creamer*
*          1 cup powdered sugar*
*          1 pound box instant chocolate mix*

*For serving: Place ½ cup of this mix in a cup and add boiling water. Store mix in airtight container, e.g., three-pound coffee can with plastic lid.*

You might receive family honor points if you whip up a bowl of the following:

### Snow Ice Cream

*Skim off top layer of freshly fallen snow. Carefully place clean snow in large bowl. Add: 1 teaspoon vanilla, ½ cup milk, and approximately ½ cup sugar. Fold over until mixed well. For an added treat, put a few drops of food coloring, and mix.*

Nutritious? No. Fun? Yes.

Snow days are fun. You'll wonder where to store all those special snow play clothes until it snows again, but you'll find a place, "You always do, mom." "Thanks for helping me have so much fun today."

This young school-oriented individual will have a tendency to overdo in any activity. Sleeping habits are so significant at this age. The success of his day—as well as yours—will depend on a sufficient amount of rest. A rushed morning is a bad start for any day. His looking forward to bedtime will depend on your attitude. If your child can expect an "end of the day" talk with you or a chapter read aloud from a favorite book, he may begin looking forward to bedtime as something pleasant and not mandatory.

You have realized the importance of an annual physical check-up to ensure good health. There are two areas that may take some observing. If you notice your child sitting too closely to the television set, holding his schoolwork close to his face, squinting, or holding his head back in an effort to focus, it may be an indication he needs glasses.

Does your child seem to ignore you when you call him—or could he be experiencing a hearing problem? Bring this to the attention of the school nurse and ask that a hearing test be administered. A slight physical handicap, detected early and corrected, could mean a more successful student.

The days of activity go on. You have taken time to create healthy forms for physical development. Even though you have been exhausted many times, you may dread seeing the elementary years end.

## HIGH SCHOOL

There is not another stage in physical development when changes will be so extreme and varied as in the teen-age years. Although highly exaggerated, one dad said, "I'm just glad his breathing is automatic, or he may stop doing that, too!" It may be taking every ounce of energy just for that teen to grow.

All the training in good eating habits will culminate at this age. You can evaluate your past years of work now. If he eats the school lunches without too many complaints, doesn't question what is served at home, and has developed a taste to try new ideas in cooking, give yourself a grade of excellence.

Instead of inventing games to get your child to eat, you will question if he will ever *stop* eating. While you are getting the table cleared from one meal, don't be alarmed if he says, "Mom, I'm still hungry." There is nothing wrong with in-between snacks as long as they do not interfere with his appetite for the next regular meal. Milk shakes, cheese and peanut butter sandwiches, ice cream, peanuts, popcorn, or a bowl of fresh fruit kept within reach make nourishing snacks. Although a sixteen-year-old eats a good breakfast, he may find it impossible to go until lunch without some type of carry-over. Give him a candy bar for a quick intake between classes at school.

These are times of fast growth in his muscles and bones. In planning your daily menus, load them with plenty of proteins, vitamins, and minerals. Your home extension agency could again assist you in free pamphlets that reveal the values of certain foods.

Choose one weekday for him to be responsible for preparing a meal. You will be pleased at his ability and creativity now that he needs less guidance. Have general cookbooks on hand and your own index file of personal recipes if he wants to try a family favorite. Now it will be in order for you to compliment *him!*

Most of his physical activity will be peer-group oriented, but don't miss out on any opportunity when you get a special invitation from your teen to go bike riding, swimming, golfing, playing on the neighborhood baseball team, substituting as a player in volleyball or, "Mom, let's go out for awhile and play pitch and catch." Now you begin making time and self available. Don't let a sinkful of dirty dishes or "I mustn't break into my daily routine" hold you back. You won't be taking time, but inventing extra time, to spend with this very young adult.

Through his elementary years he enjoyed learning the rules of games, but now he will be concentrating on developing his skill in various sports. Encourage the opportunities in intramural sports, gymnastics, baseball leagues, swim teams, tennis, or any event provided by his school or city clubs. If enough enthusiasm is shown, it may help to invest in private lessons for at least one summer.

Teens will always find ways of getting together, but they may run out of ideas for group fun. The best times they will remember will be when you took time to give a suggestion, and they took over from there. Many activities do require physical strength. There are two books available written specially for youth, which are excellent resources for get-togethers. Take time now to order them for your home library. *Ideas,* Youth Specialties, 861 Sixth Avenue, Suite 411, San Diego, California. *Funtastics,* by Louis O. Inks. Address: A Division of G/L Publications, Glendale, California.

Harvey and his wife, Annie, gathered a group of teen-agers one Saturday and took them to a farm. Harvey had gone the day before to check out different names of weeds, wild flowers, and old farm machinery left standing in the field. When he got the group on location, he told them they were going on a different kind of hike. They were to walk, but at the same time they must listen to what he had to say. He pointed out the names of weeds, wild flowers, and explained the use of the farm machinery. After about one-half mile, he stopped, had the group count off by threes and gave each group a paper. On this were listed items he had talked about. They were to retrieve each of these objects (farm machinery excepted!), which included a yellow butterfly—the fields were filled with them—bring them to a certain area and form a nature arrangement. The running and hunting began instantly. The group later settled down and worked out their nature findings. Their day ended with a teen-ager's delight: charcoaled hamburgers, baked beans, potato chips, Cokes, and roasted marshmallows. This took the complete day out of the life of a mom and dad, but they will tell you that it was a day of great satisfaction when they watched and listened to the comments around that campfire.

Most parents have their own accepted way of dealing with the important phase of the physical developmental idea toward sex. This knowledge is as essential as the food you serve and the physical activities you make available. We cannot fully understand and work with our teen-agers if we do not take time to know the frustrations and growing pains they have regarding sex. A thirteen-year-old cannot be asked to sit down and be presented with the whole idea of sex in one day. In the "Social Development" chapter of this book under PRESCHOOL, Terry began teaching her child when he was three. She made it become a natural, logical part of life—not set apart, but blended into everyday living.

There have been many books written on this subject to help the parent who wants to take time to use her own method of instruction. Since sex is a sacred trust from God and a Christian mother views it as such, she will want to mention why God instituted sex. "So God created man in his own image . . . male and female created he them. And God blessed them, and God said unto them, Be fruitful, and multiply, and replenish the earth and subdue it" (Gen. 1: 27-28).

The book *Understanding Youth,* by T. Garvice and Dorothy Murphree, is a very practical, knowledgeable, fast-reading book. In Appendix A of the book these authors stress the Biblical view of sex, the youth's attitude toward sex, and social acceptance of sex.

There may be a time when you will receive an

invitation from school to view a film on "growing up" with your junior high student. Cancel all other appointments and take time to go. This is an important time in the life of your child. It is new and could be frightening. (The "Social Development" chapter in this book discusses how vital open communication must be at all ages for all subjects.)

Mrs. Jean Stanford, a high school biology teacher, has made many observations in her classes. She finds it beneficial to encourage her students to be at ease in using correct reproductive terms. The word *vagina* becomes a natural term and thought of in the correct connotation. She suggests if your child comes home and tells you something he has learned in this area, ask him if he has learned it from a good source and if so, "Why is it a good source?"

It is of interest to find that the most knowledgeable students she has on this subject are those who attend church regularly, are active in scouting, or get their information "straight from home." She suggests a series of sex lectures be given by a competent physician or a registered nurse. This could be arranged through the church or with scout leaders.

There are free medical film services in most cities. If you know of other parents interested in presenting the subject of sex acceptably to their teen-ager, look at the film catalog's description of each film and choose the one you feel would be most beneficial in your situation. If you do not have a film projector, check out one from the public library. Call your group together, view the film, and have an open discussion. When parents realize they are in similar situations, it can be a very profitable time.

You are so busy during these years that it takes some imagination on your part to see that your child has transformed into an adult. But there he is. Active, creative, competitive, successful, inquisitive, but also secure in the knowledge that although he hasn't needed your guidance as much during his teen years, you have been there and have made yourself available. That's all he has hoped you would do.

# Take Time to Develop

## *"favor with God"*

Spiritual training of a child: when and where do you begin, mom? You must come to that time soon after the child's birth when you are fully aware, as a parent, that you are responsible in giving your child completely to the Lord. Then begin the responsibility with God's help to guide your child to "increase in favor with God" (Luke 2:52b). It will be your natural maternal instinct to feed and clothe your baby properly, but keep this thought in mind at all times—you are helping that child to "grow in grace, and in the knowledge of our Lord and Savior Jesus Christ" (II Peter 3:18a) every day he is under your care.

I am convinced that prayer is the answer to raising a family. If you will take time for this added ingredient, lifting your children's names in prayer from the first day of birth, your home is going to be unique, set apart for special things. Praying takes first priority in your life, mom. Maybe you don't feel that you have five free minutes to pray. What is wrong with praying while you feed your baby, fold diapers, straighten the house, get some ironing done, prepare a meal? Let your baby hear you pray. It becomes a simple, relaxed way of life that he will adopt for his own adult life. Talking with God seems to make it easier to talk to children. After you have taken time from your busy day to talk to God, this act itself has revealed to you how important it is to communicate with your children. Psychologists say that if you take time to listen to your children when they are two years old, you will not have a communication gap in the teen years. I am also convinced that if your children learn to talk to God in their early years, they will never have the problem of praying and then wondering whether He is listening and hearing what they say.

God promises, "I will go before thee and make the crooked places straight" (Isa. 45:2a). He is with you when you lose sleep with a sick child, when you burn a meal, break dishes, and when you are impatient with your children. He goes with you when you are feeling anxiety, experiencing stress, or facing financial difficulties. He helps you say no to many outside activities that may deprive you of giving valuable time to your family.

The Lord makes those crooked ways straight when you begin wondering, "Have I been a good mother today? Have I really done my best? Where did I fail today? Will I be able to make it through tomorrow?" Yes, time will be yours for everything that needs to be done. "God shall supply all your needs according to his riches in glory by Christ Jesus" (Phil. 4:19).

A virtue found in your life as a Christian mother is your faith in God—faith to trust in One who will guide you through each day at a time. How will you teach your children to trust? You don't rush, force, or push this teaching on your child.

Teaching trust is:

> You, as a mother, present to your child that immorality is wrong—then you trust.
> You tell him to love others—then you trust.
> You teach the importance of prayer—then you trust.

*You tell him he is responsible to God, himself, and others—then you trust.*

*You show him how to be helpful—then you trust.*

*You demonstrate love—then you trust.*

*You give each young life to Christ—then you trust that He will use this life to make his world a better place.*

In all these ways of trusting, you, as a mother, must remember to keep your childlike faith, too.

Below are instances of how God can be real in your child's life.

# INFANCY

How are you going to let your baby know about God's love? The most simple and beautiful way is communicating your own love to your baby. "God is love" (II John 4:16a). God has told us He will supply our needs; and that is exactly what you do when you keep your baby comfortable, feed him properly, bathe him, sing to him, hold him close, and speak softly to him. It is a big world he has entered, but you are the one that spells security amid all the complexities.

It is not too soon to hold your baby and say a short prayer of thanksgiving before you feed him. A church nursery worker made a practice of this before she fed each baby. One baby would not take his bottle until after the prayer was offered. No age is too young to know about prayer.

Placing a picture of Jesus in the crib and softly saying, "Jesus," in time will have a special meaning to your baby. "Let the little children come to me. . . ." (Luke 18:16a TLB).

When your baby is old enough to sit in a high chair at meals, place him between you and your husband, each of you holding hands while the blessing is being offered. It will not be long until your baby will be jabbering with you. This practice of praying will be carried on through life. As your child gets older, it will be very natural to have a prayer at each meal.

Show your little one the sunrises and sunsets; then quote a Scripture verse such as, "He hath made everything beautiful in his time" (Eccles. 3:11), or "I will lift up mine eyes unto the hills from whence cometh my help, my help cometh from the Lord who made heaven and earth" (Ps. 121:1-2). Tell your baby that God made that sunrise or sunset. Tell him God made the colored leaves, animals, clouds, and the grass. He may not respond at the time, but later you will ask, "Who made the leaves? Who made the dog? Who made the grass?" Don't be surprised when he answers, "God." The wonderful thing about being young is being able to accept eternal values.

It is quite difficult to get a young, growing family to church each week. Mom, you will need to take time the night before to make sure those little white shoes are polished, the socks have mates, the diaper bag is equipped, and that you have a vague idea of what you will prepare for your Sunday lunch. When you are running late, the baby is not cooperating, you run your stocking as you are going out the door, it's raining, and the house is a disaster area, look up! The Lord sees you are trying and that you want to give valuable training. A quiet time of meditation awaits you after your baby is settled in the nursery. While you are worshiping, your baby is receiving a supply of spiritual discipline that will last a lifetime. Later when he graduates to the toddler room, he will learn to "love one another" (Rom. 13:8b) while he is trying to live successfully with his small peers. He will learn to "be ye kind" (Eph. 4:32) when he tries to take a toy from someone, or when he pushes or bites his adversary. These are not instantaneous lessons. They are learned over and over, and the lessons are learned well because you took time to put your child in the kind of atmosphere to grasp some basic spiritual truths—to love God and man.

# PRESCHOOL

You must decide for yourself when it is time to begin training your preschooler to join you in the worship service. Some churches have special services for children up through sixth grade, but you may choose to have your child worship with you.

A visit to the church the week before his first church service may prepare your young worshiper for the following Sunday. Show him the sanctuary, the choir loft, the organ, the piano, the offering plates, and pews. If you have an overly active child (these are tomorrow's leaders), you may have to use some imagination. Your child may be like one particular pastor's child. Daddy was preaching and noticed some movement at the side of the auditorium. Without changing any inflection of his voice, he simply stated, "Billy, get out of the baptistry, your daddy's preaching." (To relieve you, dear reader, the baptistry had no water in it.)

Your child may be perfectly content to sit and observe, but most children find it almost impossible to sit for one hour. Mothers have found it effective at the beginning to bring their children in for only a portion of the service. Children are good listeners even while engaged in a small activity. This may require a larger purse, but the dividends are satisfying. Some ideas that may be used just for this one weekly occasion are miniature puzzles (ten small pieces), notebook reinforcement stickers to be stuck on a small piece of black construction paper in any kind of abstract design. A pen that changes colors is very intriguing to a small child. A piece of gum may be refreshing for that uptight moment. These suggestions are invaluable only if they are kept for the church-going experience. Use your discretion about objects to take. Some children may proclaim this a Feast Day if Mom stocks her purse with peanut butter and cracker sandwiches, Crackerjacks, dry cereal, and water. Can you imagine the distraction experienced by those sitting around these individuals? The rule of the day may be: any activity conducive to a *quiet* worship time.

Many young homes are finding ways to have effective family worship. You might hear such comments as: "Let's hurry up." "I have lessons to do." "I know you're going to pray for ten minutes." "I can't think of anything to pray about." One evening after dad had finished reading a lengthy Scripture passage, one of the older children said, "Well, that was the Old Testament; tomorrow night, the New Testament." Do not let these comments discourage you; consider them a challenge to help the children be eager for this special time of the day.

The child's spiritual growth begins reaching maturity when he realizes that in prayer hangs the balance of hope when all other hope is gone, peace when all about him is confusion, and when a commitment to total dependence on God is experienced.

When the Bible is opened for family worship, the preschooler might be allowed to hold the Book while one of the family members reads. Using different Bible translations may clarify some of the reading. Let him be responsible for getting the Bible and bringing it into the group and then putting it back in its proper place. This brings a feeling of participation and satisfaction.

On our table is a miniature loaf of bread with the words "Bread of Life" printed on it. Inside the loaf are small Scripture cards. Before the evening meal, a card is chosen, preferably by a smaller child, and handed to another to read. Some of these verses have become favorites of our children.

Very young children have a habit of praying for everything on the table, every relative, and every friend. This is not wrong and should not be treated as being funny or entertaining. As their world grows, their concerns grow. Instead of praying, "Thank you for grandma," they may add, "keep her from feeling lonely." "Thank you for my uncle. I don't want him to be sad because he is blind." These children are beginning to see that God can help in any of life's situations.

There are many things you might include in your worship—Scripture reading, prayer, songs, or discussion. You might let a bulletin board be the central location for family worship, to be changed each month. Each time you have your time together, add something to the scene on the board. You may want to suggest a family activity together for each month to accompany the worship. Here is a year of ideas for family worship. A bulletin board can be made at very little expense. We made ours from materials purchased at a lumber yard. It was hung in our kitchen so it could be seen at various times during the day.

## JANUARY

Make a snow scene. Cut out a snowman to represent each family member. (Let the children always work with you in creating each new scene.) Add something to the snowman after each family worship: eyes, nose, mouth, hat, broom, pipe, neck scarf, ears, and so on. You may want to put the completed snowmen up at first, and after each worship service add a paper snowflake in the sky. Patterns for the snowflakes can be found in a *World Book*.

## FEBRUARY

Make a picture of a pretty valentine box. Place valentines, made by each member of the family, around the box, one each day. A discussion may be held about love and why we should show love in the home and to others. The Bollinger family makes Valentine's Day a special occasion. The children help make a heart-shaped cake and set the table with the best china. After the evening meal each member is given his turn to say "I love you" to the other family members. What a natural way to verbally express love for others. For a family project the valentines made during the month could be mailed or delivered personally to special friends or to shut-ins.

## MARCH

Cut out pictures of boys and girls from an old catalog. Put the figures on the bulletin board. Tape a string to each cut-out and tape the end of the string in the sky. Each day add a kite. A nature walk may be planned by the family to observe the beginnings of spring.

## APRIL

Divide the bulletin board into halves. On one side place rabbits, baskets, eggs, and on the other side the Biblical resurrection story. Each family member may want to decide how they would like the board to look. Add an object each day. By Easter have both sides completed.

## MAY

Make a large paper May basket. Place a homemade flower in the basket each day after the family worship. The family may cooperate in making baskets and delivering them to a friend or relative along with a freshly baked package of cookies. This could become an annual family event.

## JUNE

Have green construction paper at the bottom of the bulletin board. Each day add a flower, tree, clouds, butterflies, animals—anything to do with Creation. On the last day, have each member "draw" himself from small pieces of paper. Add these to the scene. A worthwhile project is to let each person have a small plot of ground to have a flower garden. While this progresses, talk about the way God wants us to enjoy the earth. Encourage each person to care for his own garden. When the garden yields its first flowers, take a bouquet to someone who means much to the family. The children may want to place a small bouquet on the kitchen table to remind them of that month's special family worship.

## JULY

Put a string across the bulletin board. Add a paper-made firecracker to the string after each service. Later you might discuss the importance of American independence and the Christian's civic responsibility.

## AUGUST

Cut out a picture of a basket and add a paper red apple each day. The words "Apple for the Teacher" or "An apple a day keeps the doctor away" could be placed at the top of the bulletin board. The family might express their appreciation for school teachers and the work of doctors. There could be a discussion of the care of our physical bodies and the obligation we have in keeping the body well. (If older children are present this would be an ideal time to discuss the harmful ways a person could destroy or misuse his body, using as the basis for the discussion, "Ye are the temple of God" (II Cor. 6:16a).

## SEPTEMBER

Cut out a large bare tree from brown construction paper. Add a colored leaf each day. Discuss the changing of nature and the Creation. A table arrangement of colored leaves, nuts, late blooming wild flowers, and pretty rocks could be made by the children and put on display during the month.

## OCTOBER

Each night place a small paper pumpkin (have the children draw and cut out the pumpkins and put different expressions on them) around construction paper cornstalks. You may like to cut out a jack-o'-lantern and set it on a small table in front of the bulletin board. Light the candle each night during family worship. Place an open Bible by the pumpkin.

## NOVEMBER

Cut out a turkey without tail feathers. Let the children use a pattern for the feathers and add brightly colored ones to the turkey after each worship session. During the month the Thanksgiving story of the Pilgrims and Indians could be told, bringing out love for all races and emphasizing brotherly love. Your family may consider inviting a family over to enjoy Thanksgiving dinner with you.

## DECEMBER

Fill the bulletin board with dark blue construction paper. Make a silhouette of the city of Bethlehem (old Christmas cards may be used as a pattern). Add a star to the sky each evening. It is very impressive to take the children outside to let them observe the stars and imagine how the wise men felt when they saw the star that led them to Bethlehem. Again, using a small table in front of the bulletin board, the children may like to make a display of holly and a candle by the Bible and have the Book opened to the Christmas story. This is an excellent month to discuss the meaning of Christ's birth. There should be a family project of doing something very special for someone outside the home.

Mom, you can see all of this takes time; but after

studying these activities, can you visualize the lessons being taught? You are actually doing constructive activities with your family. They are recognizing your interest and concern.

Most church denominations have home devotional guides to be used each day. You may want to use your own ideas for family worship. If you do choose a specific guide, many times it will be seasonal for each particular month. Contact your church office if you are not familiar with the literature published. You will find most church leaders very helpful if they feel you are interested in setting up your own family worship.

The proverb "Actions speak louder than words" holds true where family worship is concerned. Follow-up activities are very effective in a child's life. Hopefully, this list of activities will get your imagination started. It just takes time.

How often should a mother take time to pray for her children? Begin by taking one minute each morning to pray for each child by name. You may never know the power that one minute will bring in the life of your child.

# ELEMENTARY

Hopefully, up to this point your child has heard you pray specifically for him. Wilma has made it a practice from the very first day of school to pray for each of her children. She takes them aside and prays with them individually. What a thoughtful way to take time with children.

Maybe you "pray without ceasing" (I Thess. 5:17). Let some of your prayers be heard by your child. Let him hear you pray when he is going to have a test at school or when he is having trouble getting along with a playmate. Have him listen when you offer a prayer of thanksgiving when he has been healed. Maybe he is afraid to start school. Show him the verse,

"What time I am afraid, I will trust in thee" (Ps. 56:3), and then pray that God will give him the courage he needs. What if he has made a special accomplishment on a report card, in a piano recital, received a scout award? Thank the Lord with him. Let him hear you pray.

A third grader who was terrified of her physical education teacher told her parents about it. They prayed with her. Later she said, "You know, Mr. Jones seems nicer for some reason." If children realize prayer is important to their parents, they will see its importance in their own lives.

Every mother should feel the need to have a short meditation by herself. There are many devotional books published specifically for young mothers. Dial-a-Devotion, a one-minute inspirational message, is available in many large cities through the telephone company. It is particularly good to listen to before you get any other family member up to begin the day or at a time when counting to ten is not the solution for the problem of the moment.

No day will be your best day if you do not begin with prayer. I find it uplifting to quote a Scripture verse as soon as the alarm clock rings.

Many families take advantage of the Christmas season to help in spiritual training. It was a memorable Christmas Eve for a first grader when she presented her own worship service.

### A Worship Service for the Home

*Listening Music (Listen to favorite carols played on the piano or record player)*

*Light a candle*

*Sing: "Away in a Manger"*

*Story of the first Christmas: Let child tell the story as he heard it at church or beforehand have mother read the story from Luke 2:8-17 and have the child tell it in his own words. Then have another older family member read the story from Luke 2:1-20.*

*Sing: Christmas carols*

*Prayer Time: Let each one in his own way talk to God.*

When the service was over, this young leader was extremely pleased. She had given her time to help her family worship. Everyone has his own way of celebrating Christmas.

Beverly, a very talented neighborhood mother, called several children together to practice acting out the Christmas story. She and the children painted one large piece of cardboard for the scenery. This served as props for the inn and manger scene. The children rehearsed each day after school. They were responsible for getting their own costumes. The day before the presentation each child made an invitation for his parents. They made simple refreshments to be served on the day of the performance. On the day of the play the parents assembled in the family room. The spotlight was turned on and the characters appeared. The well-known Christmas story was acted out, but it had a special meaning because one mother had taken time with children to let them tell the story in their own way.

The following year the same mother invited four girls to her home for another Christmas treat. She had cut out four simple dress jumpers. Each girl used reindeer patterns and drew around them with magic markers on their dresses. They sewed the seams on the sewing machine and the finishing touch was pulling a red ribbon through the neckline and putting jingle bells on the ends of the ribbon. This took time and patience, but the ecstasy those girls experienced when they wore their jumpers during the holiday season was well worth the effort.

Somehow, I feel every home should have a manger scene at Christmas no matter how ornate or simple. It may be a good idea to place Santa and all his trimmings in one part of the house and the Biblical decorations in another room. Many homes leave the

Bible open to the Christmas story during this season. Some families bake a birthday cake for Jesus and place it before the manger scene. To set the mood for Christmas morning, our family has a candlelight dinner on Christmas Eve, with carols as background music.

The Collins family enjoys sharing at Christmas. Weeks before Christmas, every member bakes all sorts of delicacies. On Christmas Eve they place the baked items on pretty trays covered with cellophane. They pack the back seat of their car, and as a family they deliver these gifts to special friends. It is delightful to see the children going to the various homes. I have often wondered who was receiving the greater joy.

A custom was started by the Lamars when their family was young. Each year the mother would buy or make each child a new ornament for the Christmas tree. The children would mark them so they would always know which ones were theirs. As the children grew older, they had a large assortment of ornaments. When the children married and began their own homes, the mother presented them with their box of ornaments in the hope that as they decorated their tree, they would remember the carols, the prayers for each other, and the special candlelight service they had planned after decorating the tree each Christmas. Building spiritual memories cannot be measured.

Wilma's child had a dilemma. He was born December 25. She wanted him to feel it was an honor and not a liability to be born on the celebrated day of Jesus' birth. She told her son when he was small to choose a day in December other than the twenty-fifth when he wanted to celebrate his birthday. This was a very simple thing but very important to the boy. This mother had taken time to consider and do something about her son's problem.

There will be times when you will not know how much you have done through your prayers and daily living. Have the lessons been caught and learned by your children? Then one day by your plate at the meal table is a homemade Mother's Day card. The message reads:

> *"Thank you for wanting to be my mother. Thank you for making our home so happy. Thank you for loving daddy. Thank you for being home when I come home from school. Thank you for caring for me. Oh! I could go on but I'll just say thank you for everything. Love, Pam."*
>
> *"And now abideth faith, hope, love, these three, but the greatest of these is love"* (I Cor. 13:13).

This love that you have tried to live and teach begins showing signs of growing into something positive and vital during the later elementary years. There are outward signs of compassion expressed verbally only the way a child can express them.

Beth was sitting with me one evening while we had a snack before bedtime. As we finished she said, "I just have this warm feeling around my heart. I want to keep it the rest of my life." That morning I had prayed, "Lord help me to take time with my children today to show them the goodness of your love, no matter how small my job may seem at the time." A simple, instinctive action such as taking time to have a snack with one child helped her express security in her home.

# HIGH SCHOOL

As your child promotes into junior and senior high school, you had better put aside a box of memories. It will be filled with the secret thoughts of each child. There are remembrances of love that you have taught because you realized it took time to pray and live those prayers before your children. No book has ever been published that carried any more precious thoughts than these:

"I hope you have a really lovely Mother's Day because you are the most deserving, beautiful, understanding mother in the whole wide world. Thank you for so much love. I love you more than I can ever tell you, Mother."

"Have a special Easter. I love you very much."

"To my favorite Mom. Love ya."

One night during family devotions our daughter prayed that the family would not only show more love to outsiders but also that we would show more love within our home. Each evening after that prayer my husband and I began praying together for each girl. We spoke their names and we prayed specifically for their needs. There was a tremendous change in the atmosphere of our home. We could only explain it through this act of prayer. Not only did we pray each evening but we also made it a practice to pray at breakfast for each of the girls, that God would be real to them in every experience—good or bad—for that day. One day Pamela went to her history class. The topic of Christianity was brought up and denounced by her teacher. Disagreeing, Pamela raised her hand before the teacher had finished expounding on the subject. She looked around the room and noticed her friends' hands were up, too. She took the floor and stated firmly her argument and affirmed her faith before the teacher and her class. This incident did not get into the headlines, but it made an impression on a young life. It had all started with a simple prayer at a meal—a prayer that had fully prepared her for that specific hour.

Prayer is the open door to spiritual training for any family. It is available at any hour. "God was with me today, mom." I knew our daughter had stayed up late studying for a test, but time went by and she could not finish. The next day after the children left for school I prayed, "Lord, Pam has tried; so let the things she has learned flow freely from her mind." After school she said the music professor had given them study time in band, there were no physical education classes, and she also used her lunch hour to complete her studies. "I know it won't always work out this way, but it surely did today." She had tried and the Lord had not left her lacking. She would not do it again, intentionally; but I feel the Lord knew her needs and they had been fulfilled.

There are indirect ways of teaching your teens spiritual truths. Books lying in convenient places are quite effective. Making these books available in this manner is better than saying, "I'd like you to read this. I think it could mean much to you." An introduction like this won't get the first page read. Discussion is best when your teen-ager is rested, free of pressure from school activities, and in a fairly quiet atmosphere.

I did not realize it until recently, but when Dana was thirteen, she began going with her preacher-student dad to his weekend pastorate just to be able to spend some time with him by herself. The church provided a small trailer. Dana took charge of keeping the trailer clean and cooking the meals. She and her dad had no set schedule. She cleaned when she felt like it and fixed the meals when her stomach demanded food. She took long walks in the woods and absorbed the countryside before having to come back to the city. Recently she said, "I felt closer to God on those weekends than I ever did before." ("Be still and know that I am God" [Ps. 46:10] ). How often we make the mistake as parents of thinking we have to talk all the time to teach lessons.

Spiritual life during the teen years may seem to take a back seat for some. Do not become overly concerned if church doesn't take first place for a while. These are years of endless activities. Blessed is the parent who can keep up. Doing things takes precedence over lecturing or teaching. Why not get a group together and adopt an underprivileged family? The welfare office has numerous names of children, not especially needing material things, just attention and love. Find out when the children's birthdays are and give each one a birthday party. You would be surprised how many of these children have never had a party in their honor. Ask these children to list some things they have never done but would like to do—picnics, skating, bowling, baseball. One small child asked if she could cook something. One of the teens picked her up on Saturday and they spent the afternoon baking and icing cupcakes. All of these things take time, but it is Christianity in action. Maybe your teens have been driving for a short time. Give them the responsibility of taking an older person for a ride in the country. This is a concrete way of using their new driving ability.

I am aware that young people this age have a difficult time expressing themselves; but I have kept notes, letters, and cards through the years that have shown me how very deep are the feelings and desires of young people. No family spends many days without frustrations. No matter how well a day is planned, there comes the inevitable day when tempers get the best of us; but even out of disagreements and disharmony we can relate the outcome as a result of the teaching of spiritual truth. Saying "I'm sorry," in love, will bind two people closer together.

*Mother,*

*I haven't showed it too much this morning, but I really love you a whole lot. It seems like every morning at 7:30 I always get mad; but when I do, try not to let it bother you. When I get on the bus in the mornings, I really feel bad because of how I acted. That's just the way I feel right now.*

*Please be thinking about me today. I need lots of help on my tests. And I promise you, I'm not gonna cheat at all! I want you to have a real good day, so stay happy. I love you all the time . . . even at 7:30 each morning.*

*Love,*
*Me*

I feel that compassion is one of the greatest virtues that must be instilled by example. Every mother who takes time not only with her family, but also with others, teaches concern for others throughout life. A mother prays for opportunities to open each day; she takes those opportunities with no thought of the value or rewards of the outcome. And then one day it happens:

Mom,

Ever so often I take you for granted, but not today! Lately I see that I have the greatest mother that ever was or that I could ever hope to be. When I felt such a load the other day and thought I would die if I didn't get some help, you came to my rescue. I'll always be grateful for the ways you care for me. I could never ask for a better mother than you. I dearly love you, mom. I thank you for loving me the way you do.

So on this special day it is more appropriate than ever to tell you how wonderful I know you are. You've never let me down, and I hope I can do my best to never let you down either, because I love you so much.

Love,
Your daughter

Compassion in action. There is no better way to express God's love.

Have you ever thought of getting high school young people together to go Christmas caroling through town or through the hospital corridors? They may even want to give appropriate gifts to the younger patients. And remember, just to see a young face thrills those in the geriatrics ward.

Any parent can present an idea, and this age group can settle down and put the plans together. How about campouts or a retreat from the fast teen pace? Even Jesus felt a need to get away from the crowds at times. I have known parents who have prepared banquets through their church in honor of those graduating from high school, to show the group how they have been appreciated through the years.

Any activity, any thought provoked, which shows in an indirect way that Christian living is vital, exciting, and full of hope, induces sharing these same thoughts and actions with others. The young people become aware of the good and the bad, and how they can cause good things to happen through praying diligently and taking time to make things happen.

The teen needs the personal touch, the availability of adults, and patient understanding through their eyes.

# AFTER GRADUATION

What a time of mixed feelings! Although you will want to keep your family together as long as possible, there is that day of college departure.

For a keepsake graduation present we gave our daughter a symbolic ring. The set included the birthstones of each family member, and in the middle was a tiny diamond chip representing Christ, the center and everlasting member of our home. Today we still receive hurriedly written notes saying, "Pray for me at 10:00, I'm having a major test." "I'm feeling a little away from God, and I don't like that feeling." "We've begun praying together after each date. It's the only way." "Could you send me that new translation of the Bible? My roomie read mine and really likes it. I'd like for her to have one, too."

The days of spiritual training go on and on. Why did I take time to show my children the sunsets? Why did I take time to get us all off to church when it would have been easier to stay at home? Why did we take time to continue family worship when no one seemed interested? Why did I continue to pray during those difficult hours of problems with those teen-agers? The following letter will show you why, mom.

*(A letter to a special Friend)*

Dear Friend,

I just want to write this letter to tell you some things I believe you already know. I know you understand that I need all the help you are giving me. I'm glad when you come over to me in my silent lonesome times. I'm specially grateful when you go with me into those dreaded places I enter each day. Thank you for those whispered words of encouragements.

Why are you so tricky? Sometimes I look so hard for you. Perhaps I'm not really sincere, because I can't find you at all. I cry.

You're not only my friend but my mother's friend, too. I know because I see that some of your kindness has rubbed off on her. Thank you for sharing it.

Each time I wish I had a letter to read all I have to do is go to that big stack of letters you wrote me. They are so great! I really love that present you gave me. It's exactly what I want the most. Thank you for that beautiful gift of dreams and for putting in the reality with them.

You're my closest friend, God. Thank you.

> Your daughter's love,
> Just me,
> Pamela

# Take Time to Develop

## *"favor with man"*

Mom, you are going to give your child his first actual experience of living with another individual. Will his social training be essential? It will be if you consider that everyone with whom he comes into contact will influence his life in some way. It will be essential if you know it is your responsibility to prepare your child to live successfully with others. "If it be possible, as much as lieth in you, live peaceably with all men" (Rom. 12:18). It will be important, if you are aware that wholesome social living stems from the kind of love that has its beginnings in his home.

He will be involved with people all his life. He will love and enjoy some; others he will fear and distrust. All his emotions will revolve around people individually and society as a whole. No person has the capacity to live successfully apart from people.

His introduction to people normally follows in this sequence: mom, dad, family, peers, and other adults. You are at the top of his list. You are his leading lady. You will be his first friend and helper. You have given him his physical birth into this world; now you will be the first one to teach him how to live a profitable life.

# INFANCY

You and your baby will be spending a great deal of time together during his first three months. He will hear a voice—your voice—for the first time in his life. He will feel your touch. Even though you are unsure of his reaction when you bathe him, talk to him and massage him gently with lotion or powder. Wrap him in a soft clean blanket; hold him close as you give him a meal of warm milk. This sounds routine, doesn't it? You say, "Any mother can do this." But these are minute beginnings of social development. They must not be neglected! The kind of relationship you establish at birth will affect all of your child's other social relationships.

Enjoy your role as his main character. You are his only interest. His price? Being fed and burped, kept dry and warm, cuddled, rocked, talked and sung to. With all this in his favor he will find pleasure in later social relations.

When does your baby's first social response actually occur? It is his smile—a genuine, unrehearsed smile. Every mother waits for this just as she waits to feel that first tooth. His smile will show you his pleasure and his capacity to respond to human love and care. That smile is saying, "Mom, you're doing a great job taking care of me. Thanks."

When your baby is between four and six months old, place him in the center of a large bed. Have dad or another family member lie beside him and sing or talk softly. His ears pick up sounds of love. It is a pleasant experience. This simple act creates a good social relationship with other family members.

When your baby begins crawling, you might, at times, create this social activity. Place obstacles between your baby and a desired object. He will eventually learn to push away the obstacles to get the object. This activity helps prepare him to push aside "social" obstacles he may face in the future.

Very soon he will begin to jabber. In his crude talking attempts he might expect a response from you. "Is that right?" "That's good." "That sounds interesting." Look at him while he is talking. Edith's two-year-old pulls his mother's face around to his and says, "Talk to me, mom." When Tammy's boys want something, she tells them, "You must use words." She is helping them to communicate with her and others.

Talking and listening to this young one cannot be overemphasized. If you will realize the significance of this communication with your child by the age of two, and let it be a continuing experience, it is likely there will not be a gap in the troublesome teen years. Remember: *take time to listen!*

It is extremely important that you have a variety of ways to have constant close contact with your child during his first year. A day care center cannot be a substitute for you, mom. Some mothers do find it necessary to work away from home. If so, try to spend your lunch hour with him. In favorable weather have a quick picnic together. If he eats his lunch before you get him, then spend your time together and go to a park and play for a while. Go to a drive-in for refreshments or take a short ride or walk together.

If it cannot be worked out to be with each other at noon, as soon as you get home from work take time to do any of these activities just mentioned. You may want to hold him and read. None of this sounds too outstanding, but later it will play a vital factor in his mental health and social feelings toward himself and others.

You may enjoy eating out, but you wonder when to start teaching your young child the basics of public social graces. Sharon is the mother of twin daughters. At times she feels the need to get away from her numerous domestic tasks. She prepares the girls in advance when she decides to take them out for a brief time. "Girls, we are going out for a soda. Mother expects you to be nice. You are to stay in your seat. We will try not to spill our drinks." Because she takes time to train before attempting a new situation, her children know exactly what is expected of them. She wants times like these to be a treat and help create in them an appreciation for the thoughtful acts of other people.

Jeannie took her son out to eat. He insisted on holding his glass of water. She knew he had not yet conquered this task. "Tory, this is a big glass. You do not have any other clothes to put on if these get wet. Let mother help you." Too simple? He let go of the glass, accepted help, and both enjoyed a pleasant meal. Children will understand if you take time to keep talking with them.

A toddler is not ready to cooperate with his peers; so when you are planning that first special birthday, he may be more content to have his family or proud relatives as his guests. A two-year-old loves animals. Decorate a cake with bright plastic animals. Let him make invitations with your help. Let him choose pictures of animals or whatever theme is chosen. He can then paste the pictures on construction paper. You print the necessary information on the invitations and let him do the mailing. Your conversation with him can be made interesting during preparation time. Discuss animals, the names of the guests, the pretty cake and candles. This event will be special and will add another happy childhood memory of doing something with mom.

A child can be taught social responsibilities when he begins understanding verbal instruction. You may want to provide a drawer or low cabinet shelf in the kitchen to place some toys in order that your child may be close to you if supervision is necessary. "This place is yours. When you take your toys out, you must also put them back when you are through playing." Before Jennifer and Jill take their nap, they are expected to put their toys in the toybox. After this work is done they look forward to a read-aloud story before they rest.

Mom, take time to teach your young child to be accountable for what he does. He is responsible for certain properties and the care of them. Our society is waiting for a young citizen like this.

# PRESCHOOL

"Let's have a tea party." That preschooler will not only be pretending but also learning. In one tea party he will have established hand coordination, language communication, imagination, and a foundation for social skills.

Playing and living with others are important learning processes. Up to this age most of your child's social development has been learned with you or the other family members. Now you might consider activities that involve a peer. Some of the play will require teamwork to obtain fulfillment. Have you ever thought it would be more work to invite another child over to play? This will take little supervision and will satisfy your child's social needs. If you provide a play area and simple equipment they will entertain themselves—and for once you may have time to catch up on the ironing.

"Let's play house." Have a box containing dresses, shoes, purses, wallets, hats, ties, jewelry, and gloves. These articles may produce the most magical hours a child may have when he or she becomes "mom" or "dad." RULE: *never throw away any article that can be used to "play house."* This form of play helps children establish their sex identity and accept their role in society.

Your child has entered the "Era of Smearing." Do the words *sand, water, paste, clay, mud,* or *fingerpaints* spell the word *mess* to you? These products help establish socially approved activities. They help to redirect aggression with pounding, mixing, or drawing.

A simple wooden box or an old tractor tire makes an excellent sandbox. Suggest that your child and his guest make cakes, muffins, and a variety of desserts for a "pretend" party. Have a small table and chairs nearby for them to serve their freshly baked goods. Plastic containers and old baking pans make excellent play equipment.

Encourage the two playmates to have a "Picture Search" together. Articles needed are two magazines, two pictures with one main subject, paste or glue, construction paper, and a black felt tip pen. Cut the two pictures into four simple pieces each. Hide each piece separately in the two magazines, have the children search for the pieces, put the pictures together, and mount them on construction paper with the paste. After the pictures are dry, go around each piece with the felt tip pen to create a stained glass appearance. Be sure to hang this original art production where the family can see, and let your young visitor take his home to his family.

When you offer activities, notice the communication you create. It makes a pleasant and satisfying situation to work with someone.

Play-Doh gives excellent results. Sit with the children and work with them to make various shapes, such as squares and balls. Make a bowl or basket by rolling out a long piece of Play-Doh, coiling it around and around to the desired depth of the bowl or basket. Put a handle on the basket and fill with imaginary bird eggs, Easter eggs, or fruit. If you have time to spare, make your child and his guest "jewelry"—a ring, watch, or bracelet. You can even mold long fingernails. Leave the scene and stand unnoticed as you view a low-priced production of live television for the day.

"Mom, can we make mud pies?"(Where did they ever get that idea? Did you tell your child how *you* made mud pies when *you* were small?) Sometime in every mother's life she has come up with enough dirt and water to make mud pies. Provide either old cake pans or disposable pie pans. Give them spoons and a bowl for mixing, and show them the appropriate place for digging—otherwise some of your favorite flower bulbs may be exhumed. They will need a glass of water before the "bake-off" begins. While they are busy, provide an extra treat. Put two cups of washing powder in a large mixing bowl, add two tablespoons of water, and whip as you would whipping cream. You may need to add a few drops of water until you get the desired fluffy texture. Have the children set their pies in the sun; and when the product is almost dry, they can ice them with the whipped washing powder. You might put candles on the pies for a pretend birthday party. For a real snack, serve a cupcake and a cold drink. You have had two children working and playing under delightful circumstances, readily accepting each other as playmates.

Another activity in which two must cooperate to get the desired effect is spatter painting. Provide a square of fine screen wire, an old toothbrush, construction paper, thinned tempera paint, newspaper, and either large tree leaves or cut-out silhouettes of familiar objects. Spread the newspaper over a large area of the floor, lay the construction paper on top of the newspaper, and place the leaf or cut-out on top of the construction paper. Select one child to hold the screen wire about three inches above the picture. The other child dips the toothbrush into the paints and briskly rubs it back and forth across the screen wire. The paint spatters on the construction paper. Let him repeat this action until he is satisfied with the way his picture looks. Remove the leaf or cut-out and his picture is finished. Lay it aside to dry while the other child takes his turn. These two children will remember this day for a long time. They have worked together to create something very gratifying.

Dana's dad made her a small cabinet with a sink. The sink was a square cake pan that could easily be removed. Dana would invite a friend over, and when they played "house" her mother would put warm soapy water in the sink so the girls could clean the play dishes and set the table. Eventually the play was transferred into helping her mother with the family dishes. Dana learned where to put the silverware and how to dry some of the nonbreakable dishes. Later, she and her mother found a picture of a proper table setting. Dana studied the picture, and by looking at it she was able to set a table for the evening meal. She was learning to cooperate by working with her mother, and was realizing a feeling of usefulness to her family.

Birthday parties are excellent opportunities for social training. Carrie loved her Raggedy Ann doll, so she and her mother followed the theme of Raggedy Ann for her party. They discussed Carrie's role as hostess while they were making preparations for her young guests. When the party was over, her mother was pleased to see her daughter walk to the door with each friend and thank her for the gift and for coming to her party.

On Daniel's third birthday his mother began telling him about the day he was born. "Daniel, you looked like an Indian. You were red and had a big nose." She showed him his baby picture. Each year she adds to this story of his birth. (More is said about this in chapter II on sex education.)

"Mother, I wonder who my real parents are? I wonder what they look like?" Ann is a socially well-adjusted adopted daughter. Ann was six months old when her parents began singing make-up songs about "our little adopted daughter." Her parents also began this practice of adding events of her birth on her special day. At a very early age they would talk to her about her adoption. Later when she could talk, she would very proudly tell her friends, "I'm adopted." Because her parents started soon after birth, her acceptance seemed more natural. When she asked the questions about her real parents, her mother would answer, "Ann, your alleged father was tall like dad, and your mother had red hair and was a small woman like me. I don't know why they weren't able to keep you, but they must have loved you very much to have wanted to provide a mother and dad who could take care of you." One of Ann's favorite parts of her story was when her mother said, "We were overcome when the caseworker placed you in our arms. On the way to your new home we just kept peeking at you and loving you all the way." Margaret fixed Ann a scrapbook, one she could handle easily, to show her all the good times they had with her as a baby. The book contained pictures of the baby shower and all the gifts given because the friends were so happy for Ann and her parents. Living with such loving parents from the beginning has caused each of her growing up experiences with others to be pleasant situations.

For the older preschooler, have a project party. One boy received a new tent from his parents. When the guests arrived, they pitched the tent, had access to toys in the family room, and made their own forms of entertainment.

With all the play that comes with being four or five, there is a certain amount of work responsibility. Each mom must learn to accept less than perfection in her child's putting away toys, helping set the table, cleaning the table after a meal, drying dishes, dusting, or making his bed. If his bedspread is crooked, leave it. You will have to watch him flounder. His satisfaction is greater than yours. He lacks your years of experience, but his determination makes up for his inexperience.

The book *Growth and Development of the Young Child*, by Breckenridge and Murphy, is excellent reading for social training. The authors discuss the emotional climate of the home, the position of each family member, the middle child, and responsibilities in the home (pp. 40-46). This is used as a textbook and could possibly be found in a public library.

# ELEMENTARY

It's a new world for your first grader. For five years you have prepared him for school. Up to this point you have spent approximately 100 percent of his waking hours with him. Now he is to be introduced to a thirty-five-hour school week away from you. He will meet teachers, play with strangers, accept those who are different, tolerate discipline outside the home, abide by school rules, have someone other than his mom bandage his skinned knees and elbows, learn to hold back tears, receive grades for behavior, and if nothing else, he will learn to sit still for the first time in his active young life.

Although his school curriculum will provide playing and working with others, he will still need social contacts outside of school. You can help him build new friendships by encouraging your child to invite a classmate home. Doing homework together disguises work into fun. Get out the chalkboard and let them do their school assignments together.

You might begin making the slow exit here as the main character, but don't make that exit too soon. Talking with your child and keeping the communication lines open are still important. Try to produce an atmosphere suitable for conversation. Let your child have the experience of being with each parent alone. A mother of seven children says she has always taken time to be alone with each child. Someone once asked her, "How can you accomplish it with all you have to do?" "There are seven days in the week. Each child has chosen the one evening of the week we will spend together. I feel that each of my children is special and deserves a time when no one else is around."

Being alone with your child will help you learn what has interested him throughout the day or made him happy, sad, or frustrated. You may hear some secret thoughts. "Mom, I don't think Billy wants to be my best friend anymore!" You may need to reassure him at this point.

Depending on the weather, have a hot or cold drink waiting for him after school. Don't miss this time to sit down and hear him talk on the general subject of school; then inform him what has happened during your day. Get up ten minutes early on a spring day, encourage your child to dress quickly, fix yourself a cup of coffee and your child a glass of juice or milk, and sit outside and experience some "small" talk before it is time for him to go to school. Pass up unnecessary meetings so you can be at home in the evening. Some of your organizations are important to you, but so is your child, and he is home very little during the school year. If you can, plan your work and meetings during the day so most of your evenings will be free.

Produce play that requires teamwork with other family members or friends. Create a train that is pulling freight cars made from cardboard refrigerator boxes. Have each child responsible for making his own car. Let them go around the neighborhood inviting small children to take imaginary train rides. Have a circus complete with clowns, barkers, side shows, booths of ball throw, balloon burst, penny throw, and so on. These activities take a tremendous amount of cooperation; so organize a neighborhood get-together. Use your backyard for the noon or evening meal, ask everyone to bring covered dishes. Go to other lawns for volleyball, croquet, or badminton. If you are fortunate to live by a large open field, use all ages to play baseball. Neighborhood unity is almost extinct. Take time to make it a new happening in your child's life. There is something special about all ages playing and laughing together.

"An empty stable stays clean, but there is no income from an empty stable" (Prov. 14:4 Living Letters). This might be said of any mother who cannot tolerate a cluttered room—at times. If your child and his friends would like to put on a show indoors when the weather is unsuitable for outside play, give in; but be sure ground rules are laid concerning clean-up when the performance is over. Pam, Dana, and Beth enjoy having doll shows on rainy days. This requires costumes, lighting, props, rehearsal, judges, an audience, and applause. The most excitement is getting ready for the production.

There is something intriguing and mysterious about putting a blanket over the kitchen table as a substitute tent. Many secret clubs have been formed in this private atmosphere.

Purchase an inexpensive camera for your child to use on a group outing with friends. Suggest taking pictures of scenery and unusual poses of the group. The finished products will help him remember the good times with his friends.

Some toys and games require sharing. A walkie-talkie set is no good "without a pal." Checkers, dominoes, table tennis, and other table games demand teamwork. Double hopscotch, baseball, Flying Dutchman, and three deep call for cooperation. Play "statue." One person swings each child around, and he must stay in the position he lands. The one swinging will tell each one to express some mood such as happiness, sadness, or silliness. A judge is chosen to pick the best one, and the one chosen becomes the one to swing. This involves everyone in a social activity.

Parents are still considered important social contacts during the elementary age, with dad coming to the foreground. Watch him and your child learn to appreciate each other through a variety of ways. Have them plan a day of fishing. Let them prepare the picnic lunch, get the fishing gear together, and plan where they will go. Hand them a camera as they walk out the door so they can bring back proof of their day's catch.

Pamela and her dad look forward to harvesting walnuts together each fall from "their" tree. They sack them, sit in line to get them weighed, and then decide how the money will be spent.

Sometimes a child finds it difficult to talk with his dad—especially if something has gone wrong. Mark began telling his mother his problems and then would say, "Will you tell dad?"

"No, Mark, but I'll help you tell him." Joyce felt she needed to keep communication open between dad and child.

Children face social problems that are as complex to them as those their parents face. There are many children's stories written that have animal characters enacting human social problems without the child realizing social lessons are being taught. *Charlotte's Web*, by E. B. White is an excellent read-aloud story that shows a child how to live successfully with different personalities. *If Everybody Did*, by Jo Stover teaches a child to be thoughtful and responsible to others. Ask the children's librarian in your public library to help you find books for this learning situation.

Birthdays shared with friends become special delights to your elementary child. All children vary in the way they would like to celebrate. What about the menu? This is his day; so let him tell you in advance what he would like. Get ready! It may vary from hot dogs to steaks (in later years). He might like his birthday meal to be at the park, or cupcakes baked in ice cream cones served at school, or snowballs made by a dip of ice cream rolled in coconut with a candle in each one for his guests to make a wish with him. He may request having his special friend eat with him and his family at a restaurant.

There is a certain amount of suspense when the

guests are asked to come in costume. Paul wanted to have a pirate party. He made maps out of brown paper and hid the treasure chest in a most unlikely place. The chest contained the party favors. Each guest was asked to come dressed as a pirate, with Paul responsible for making black eye patches for each one.

Cowboy and Indian costumes are right-on. For a special treat dad might know just where he can get a gentle horse for that day and give rides during the party. A similar party would be to ask the children to come dressed in old-fashioned costumes. (Again, dad may know just the place to get an antique car to give rides.)

Alice asked each of her friends to bring her favorite doll. There were prize ribbons for the "prettiest," "oldest," "most talented," and "best all-around." Then each girl was given a ribbon to put on her favorite doll.

During their elementary years we gave our daughters a charm bracelet after they finished first grade. Each year afterward we added a charm disc. It was inscribed with the grade, name of the teacher, the year, and the school they had attended. This enabled them to remember their social relationships with that particular teacher and the friends with whom they had associated.

Every mother manages enough courage to have one bunking or slumber party in the later elementary years. If you plan well in advance, you may find it highly successful and want to do it again. This does take some supervision; but most of the planning will be in an informal atmosphere with light snacks, plenty of movement, and quiet (hopefully) conversation after midnight!

During these years you will see how important it is to help your child associate successfully with other individuals. Along with a desire for much group activity, he will also have a growing desire for some privacy. See that he gets it. Respect it. Besides his accepting others into his life, his private thoughts may be his way of accepting himself as a unique and important person. This is *his* time that he doesn't have to share, defend his rights, cooperate with or please someone else. ("What is man that thou art mindful of him?" [Heb. 2:6] ).

# HIGH SCHOOL

Think back. Only twelve years ago *you* were the only one in your child's life. You had all the answers for all the questions. Now? Exit, Leading Lady; enter, Peers.

When your child is hardest to live with because of his being so unsure of himself, you will want to take time to give sustained parental interest. "I don't think there's one teacher that likes me." "Some mornings I get up and I'm just plain ugly." "I don't have one decent thing to wear!" "Will I ever start gaining weight?" "My nose is too big!" These are some of his secret thoughts.

Your continued interest will boost his self-esteem. More than anything else he will need understanding and faith in himself. There will be times when the only help you can offer is to listen. If so, take time to do this. You will need to understand the forces that make him unstable. "That teacher is unfair to me." He will be unpredictable. "I'd rather go out with Donna instead of Cindy. Why did I ever tell Cindy I'd go with her!" One day he might accept a kiss from you and the next day he will tell you it is too juvenile.

During your child's twelfth year read some books written by reliable authors to help you in your understanding of adolescence. The book *Between Parent and Teenager* by Haim Ginott contains some very practical information. It will take much effort on your part to adjust effectively to the changes that will occur during your child's adolescent years. The type of behavior you saw in the elementary years may take a completely different course. You might even feel at times that you are living with a stranger. You're not. You are just witnessing his attempts at reaching out for adulthood. If you will take time to help him, he'll get the job done in a creditable manner.

Wholesome social relationships can be created if you are willing to take time to provide the groundwork and then to let your teen take over from there. During the summer Pamela read an article about a unique teen-age brunch. "Pam, why don't you invite some of your friends over before school starts, and serve this brunch? It will certainly be a conversation piece." Here was the idea: Serve fruit: pineapple chunks, melon balls, banana and pear slices, fresh strawberries, seedless grapes. Dips in tall glasses: whipped cream, orange juice, butterscotch sauce, lime juice, whipped cream cheese, maple syrup. Dunks in shorter glasses: chopped almonds, confectioner's sugar, chocolate sprinkles, coconut, chopped peanuts.

From this suggestion, Pamela shopped, prepared the food, chose suitable dishes, and set a beautiful candlelit table which delighted the guests. Dad hid the tape recorder and caught the conversation about the food concoctions, the new school year, and laughter. He then ran the tape back to the girls for the finishing touch of a "fruitful" social event.

Shirley presented the idea of an old-fashioned summer hayride in the country. After the ride, games of yesteryear were organized. There were sack races, three-legged races, tug-of-war, human wheelbarrow relay, and a stick relay. At the end of a most perfect day the teen-agers sat around and ate homemade ice cream and cookies.

According to the seasons of the year, take time to make your home or car available for luncheons during school holidays, chili, taco or pizza suppers, bunking parties, ball games, caroling, swimming, touch football, or anything that requires group participation. Your job will be willingness to help—when asked.

Every teen should have at least one surprise birthday party. You will need the help of a close friend who will take care of the invitations. Have some of the guests come early to set the table, blow balloons, and decide on a hiding place. For Joyce's fifteenth birthday her mother hollowed out a watermelon half and filled it with fresh fruits. This made a beautiful centerpiece accompanied with cake, ice cream, and Cokes. For games her mother used the book *Funtastics*, by Louis O. Inks.

With all this peer activity he will still have time for you. Family projects, which are social times completely unrehearsed, are excellent opportunities for working and talking together. Bob said the closest he ever felt to his dad was the time when he purchased an old car, and he and his dad worked on it together in the evenings. "I learned much about my dad I hadn't known before; and I guess he learned more about me, too."

Dana and Beth had been wanting to do something special to the family room which was decorated with early American furniture. There was a metal frame of an antique treadle sewing machine setting in the garage. "Girls, why don't we get dad to saw that frame off to the height of an end table, have him put a large square wooden top on it, and you finish it the way you want to." They liked the idea. We looked for and cut out every available old-fashioned picture we could find, and glued them in collage form over the top and sides of the table top. Next we painted over the pictures with orange shellac, then gave it a finished look with a coat of glossy varnish. After it was thoroughly dry, we measured the top and ordered a glass to preserve the finish. Not only did we make a beautiful piece of furniture but also discussed and planned together in an atmosphere suitable for a growing mother-daughter relationship.

A similar activity was carried out later with peers when Pamela did the same type of art work with her bed, dresser, and side table. She and her friends painted a nature scene on the drawers and sides of the dresser. The dresser top was a collage of pictures, initials of friends, pop songs, and contemporaneous sayings. The headboard and foot of the bed were done in the same manner. The girls spent hours talking while they worked.

Nothing will ever be quite so important as the family conversation around the meal table. It will take your imagination, ingenuity, talent, and time to have the entire family around the table for at least one meal each day. Since this doesn't come naturally, you won't have 100 percent attendance every day; but insist that this time is vital as a family and everyone is to do his best to be there. During the meal hear about your child's accomplishments and honors at school. This is also an ideal situation to give your teen a chance to give his opinions. He may want to voice a complaint about a certain family restriction. This is good. It helps him reduce his tension. Your limits are actually a comfort and a source of reassurance. You may hear, "Hey, I heard this joke at school today. . . ." Afterward everyone decides if it's a "family" joke, suitable for the public.

If your teen is having an extremely busy week at school, treat him to an early deluxe breakfast at a restaurant before school, or just go out for doughnuts. Give him an opportunity to talk about his activities and help him organize a suitable solution to get his work done. Encourage your husband to take his daughter out for a "date." Use all the formalities such as calling her on the phone to officially ask her out, dress appropriately, open the car door for her, assist her into the chair at the restaurant, and give her first choice of a menu. What follows? Conversation that would never and could never be discussed with the whole family. Take her home and let her know how good it has been to be with her. Mom, it could be just as interesting to do something similar with your son.

Even if secretly you feel it is an imposition on your time, try not to resent having to take your teen to and from school for special practices or meetings. This is an excellent time to talk with each other.

Dating will be an inevitable social event in your teen's life. Every parent must make his own decision when the child's dating should begin. Some young people enjoy having one of the parents stay up until they get home from their dates. You will hear more about the date if you do stay up. Somehow the magic has disappeared by the next day. Perhaps you just are not a "night" person. Leave a note. "Come see me before you go to bed."

Blessed is a girl's mom who has a sewing machine and knows how to use it. A teen-age girl is critical of her appearance, especially when the dating years arrive. Take time to help her shop for proper patterns and good quality material; then not only sew the garment, but also fit it to her as you sew. Your daughter will receive added assurance and feel more comfortable in well-fitted clothes. Your clothing budget may be limited. Plan to make coordinate outfits in her favorite colors. From the same pattern you may have the coordinates of a blouse, vest, jacket, short skirt, long skirt, and slacks. You may want to add a sweater to complete the ensemble. There are numerous ways she can wear this type of wardrobe.

Socially accepted morals about dating are learned through your conversations with each other. Reading books written by Christian authors can be helpful. *That Girl in Your Mirror,* by Vonda Kay VanDyke, and on the lighter side, *Mom, You Gotta Be Kiddin',* by Mary D. Bowman are excellent guides for your teen.

Every parent should have the privilege of enjoying the child's dating years. How your teen responds socially with the opposite sex will be affected by the quality of his past relationships and the kind of guidance you have taken time to give him. This will develop a belief in himself and help him approach the various problems that come with dating. His big need is your understanding.

"There is a right time for everything" (Eccles. 3:1 TLB), including a time for a teen-ager to daydream in the privacy of his room. This may be the time he will conquer personal battles. He thinks, "Should I go along with my friends or take a chance at being called 'strange' or 'weird'?" He may take this time to record in his diary. Great! But, mom, *do not enter* into the secrets of his book. He may be writing out his bad thoughts. This releases good and bad tensions in an acceptable manner. He will have memories posted all over his room to remind him of good and not so good times. Having a candle lit may help him find the solitude he needs after a frustrating day. This may be "a time to cry" (Eccles. 3:4 TLB). Try not to interrupt—unless you are asked. Crying relieves many unexplainable emotions.

On their seventeenth birthday our girls received a stereo-radio combination to be used in their rooms. When the door goes shut and the volume goes down, they have entered into their own world to find a completely satisfying experience.

In the later teen years he may show slight beginnings of feeling a responsibility for other people outside of himself. Baby-sitting brings on this responsibility for both boys and girls. Volunteer work in hospitals, visiting nursing homes, Christmas caroling to shut-ins, giving picnics for underprivileged children, having international students in the home during holidays, or making tray cards for the geriatrics wards or even getting permission to help feed the older patients—all these things satisfy basic human needs.

One Christmas a group of teens decorated the sitting room in the pediatrics ward. They made a snowman by filling a clear gallon jar with freshly popped corn. They put the remaining corn in a small fish bowl and turned it upside down on top of the jar for the snowman's head. They secured the two with masking tape, then topped it with a black construction paper hat. The eyes and mouth were also made from black paper. The snowman was completed by placing a small plaid wool scarf around his neck. They placed inexpensive wrapped gifts—such as books, puzzles, and lap games—around the snowman to encourage a faster recovery for the young patients. Here was a social act transformed into a spiritual deed, "for some who have done this have entertained angels without realizing it" (Heb. 13:2b, TLB).

Here is the abundant reward of your taking time from this one's birth to relate to him the joy of successful living not only with, but also for others. All through these hectic years you will work behind the scenes. There may be times when you will get the feeling of not being appreciated; but "be not weary in well doing" (II Thess. 3:13) for your children will "arise up and call [you] blessed" (Prov. 31:28a)—in time.

As he rushes out the door almost late for another school activity, hear what he's saying, "Thanks for letting me have friends in." "Thanks for listening, mom." Then go about your work and thank God you have taken time to help your teen enjoy living with himself and others.

# 5 | Mom, Take Time for Yourself

"Mom, aren't you lucky to have kids?" Dana, an eight-year-old, asked one day.

"Yes, I really am blessed. I enjoy playing with you. I like to see how you are growing in your spiritual life and see how curious you are about the world you live in. I also like to watch you having fun with other children."

Mom, you *are* blessed to have children; but can a mom like you see the significance of having time for yourself, time when you think of no one *but* yourself? You need moments to shut out family demands, phone calls, and ringing doorbells. Your most creative time of the day may be working out ways to have time for yourself. It makes you a more interesting wife and effective mother and at the same time helps you continue developing your own individuality.

You are like no other human being. You have read the following Scripture before, but read it now as though these verses pertained just to you.

> *Who can find a virtuous woman? for her price is far above rubies.*
> *The heart of her husband doth safely trust in her, so that he shall have no need of spoil.*

*She will do him good and not evil all the days of her life.*

*She seeketh wool, and flax, and worketh willingly with her hands.*

*She stretcheth out her hand to the poor; yea, she reacheth forth her hands to the needy.*

*Strength and honour are her clothing; and she shall rejoice in time to come.*

*She openeth her mouth with wisdom; and in her tongue is the law of kindness.*

*She looketh well to the ways of her household, and eateth not the bread of idleness.*

*Her children arise up, and call her blessed; her husband also, and he praiseth her.*

*Many daughters have done virtuously, but thou excellest them all.*

*Favour is deceitful, and beauty is vain: but a woman that feareth the Lord, she shall be praised.*

*–Prov. 31:10-13, 20, 25-30*

See how special you are? You need time alone to reevaluate your various roles. In choosing a time for yourself, you may want to be completely alone. There will be other times you will want to be associated with others.

You have already asked yourself this question: "How can I find time for myself when I feel that I'm on house call twenty-four hours a day?" As soon as you have asked this question, decide in that exact moment how you can *create* time for yourself. You are a deserving person. You have the daily responsibilities of helping your child develop mentally, physically, spiritually, and socially. These areas are necessary to you in keeping your life exciting. You don't want to endure life, you want to enjoy it.

# TAKE TIME TO MEDITATE

Every mother needs God in her day. You cannot do your best work without help from above. As soon as that alarm rings, before you get out of bed, repeat, "This is the day which the Lord hath made; we will rejoice and be glad in it" (Ps. 118:24). With that affirmation, the Lord becomes your guide. All the help you will need for this one day will be revealed to you because you felt a need to give Christ top priority. He has entrusted motherhood to you; now He is waiting to help you fulfill your role. You cannot afford to be the proverbial Martha, always doing less important things and not taking time for prayer and Scripture reading.

When can you have a meditation time? The most likely time for a mother with a young child is during his nap. In five minutes of prayerful Bible reading, you can receive the richest blessings of the day. You will be amazed at the outlook you will have on your busy schedule. You will have a new incentive for planning meals, doing the laundry, making beds, ironing, sewing, sweeping, and all the other daily jobs connected with being a housewife and mother. It is possible for you to pray while you are doing your work. Learn to "pray without ceasing" (I Thess. 5:17). Prayer may not change outward circumstances, but it will enable you to accept any challenge of that day.

If your child no longer takes naps, put him in his room during this time. Give him some books to look at or suggest quiet play with puzzles, coloring books, or other activity resources. If he has a record player, help him choose a record of music or stories. Put an alarm clock by his bed. Set it to go off between ten to fifteen minutes. Show him how to shut it off, explaining that when it rings, he may get up. See that he has a drink and has used the bathroom before you leave him, and emphasize that you are not to be disturbed during this time. Try choosing a time when your child has a favorite morning television program that will hold his interest as long as thirty minutes. Utilize some of this time for meditation.

Now, close out the rest of the world. Offer a prayer

of thanksgiving and praise and "let your requests be made known unto God" (Phil. 4:6b). Thank Him for your health that enables you to carry out your work. Praise Him for His magnificent love. Tell Him your weaknesses and how you need Him to make you strong. You might enjoy reading a Scripture passage during this time. The Bible reveals tried and true recipes for living a successful, happy life. Other suggestions for this time would be reading some hymns of faith, assurance, consecration, and service, or listening to a recording of religious music.

There are many forms of daily guides written for inspiration. Marjorie Holmes has voiced the deep feelings of many housewives in her book *I've Got to Talk to Someone, God.* Many churches give daily devotional books. Study the contents before buying them to make sure they will benefit you during your meditation time.

This will take a special effort on your part, but as you read the Bible and a certain verse speaks to you, jot it down. Place it over your sink, pin it to your ironing board, or tape it to your mirror. Read it over and over until you have committed it to memory. Listen to the spiritual wealth contained in these verses; then discover on your own how exciting it is to search the Scriptures. Without a doubt, the following verses have been written for every mother.

> *And in the morning, then ye shall see the glory of the Lord.* –Exod. 17:7a
>
> *He that dwelleth in the secret place of the most High shall abide under the shadow of the Almighty.* –Ps. 19:1
>
> *Then he said, Lo, I come to do thy will, O God.* –Heb. 10:9
>
> *Let the words of my mouth, and the meditation of my heart, be acceptable in thy sight, O Lord, my strength, and my redeemer.* –Ps. 19:14
>
> *Behold, thy servants are ready to do whatsoever my lord the king shall appoint.* –II Sam. 15:15b

*For I the Lord thy God will hold thy right hand, saying unto thee, Fear not; I will help thee. –Isa. 41:13*

*Be perfect, be of good comfort, be of one mind, live in peace; and the God of love and peace shall be with you. –II Cor. 13:11b*

*The Lord is my light and my salvation; whom shall I fear? the Lord is the strength of my life; of whom shall I be afraid? –Ps. 27:1*

*The Lord is my strength and my shield; my heart trusted in him, and I am helped; therefore my heart greatly rejoiceth; and with my song will I praise him. –Ps. 28:7*

With the following verse is this devotional thought.

*Behold, God is my salvation; I will trust, and not be afraid: for the Lord Jehovah is my strength and my song; he also is become my salvation. –Isa. 12:2*

Try to live a simple life. Do not try too hard to be perfect, but rather let your spiritual life be formed by your duties and by the actions which are brought about by circumstances. Do not think about tomorrow. Be confident in the love that God has for you and your family every day of your life.

When you "write them upon the table of thine heart" (Prov. 3:3), Scripture will come to mind in the days when you lose patience, sleep, and your sense of humor; when you burn a meal or don't feel appreciated; when the checkbook doesn't balance; and (even worse) when you receive an overdrawn bank statement.

Terry had a bad day. She couldn't go to sleep even after she had put the children to bed. Her husband listened to her talking about all the things that had gone wrong and then suggested, "Terry, why don't you get up and read some Scriptures?" At first she thought he was being facetious, but she felt she had nothing to lose. She got up, read for a short time, went back to bed, and fell asleep immediately.

When Leslie gets aggravated or becomes extremely

busy, she gets a backache. She started the practice of quoting Scripture when she felt tension building up. As she concentrated on the verses, her tension ceased and the backache was gone. "In quietness and in confidence shall be your strength" (Isa. 30:15b).

## TAKE TIME TO BE ALONE

No one can live confidently or be at peace with himself if he does not have some time alone, for one can find much pleasure in himself. Having the chance to be alone may mean getting your husband's approval and cooperation. If he is not available, find a qualified baby sitter to take care of your child if only for one or two hours.

Many mothers are being introduced to "Mother's Morning Out" sponsored by various churches. The mother leaves her child with his age group which is supervised by a qualified worker, and she has two hours each week to do whatever she pleases. Can you visualize what all you could do during this time? Once a month the mother takes her turn in taking care of the children, but the other mornings are free.

There are four mothers who each have a preschool child. Once a week one of the mothers is responsible for caring for the four children. While the emancipated mothers are enjoying some deserved time alone, their children are at the public library listening to the weekly story hour. Afterward they are taken out for refreshments or to the park to use the play equipment.

Many cities have organized Newcomer's Clubs which provide baby-sitting services. Since it is sometimes difficult to locate a good baby-sitter when your family has moved into an unfamiliar situation, the club provides a mother the chance to build up baby-sitting hours. If she keeps a group of children for three hours, then she is entitled to three hours of baby-sitting from one of the other members.

All of these ideas are suggestions to help you take time alone. This could help you to continue being the unique person that you are. Now you can indulge and humor your own interests.

For a starter, begin by simply reading the daily newspaper or a magazine article without one interruption. Choose a room in the house, close the door, and you will feel strangely satisfied when you have accomplished this simple action without anyone around.

Taking a walk alone during a spring or fall day can be mentally, physically, and spiritually invigorating. Some mothers feel refreshed by planning a weekly appointment with a beautician. When you are buying the weekly groceries, concentrate on staying with the list you have accumulated through the week; buy store brand names; go immediately after you have eaten a meal, and—go alone. It is a fact that you can stay within your food budget if you put this practice into effect. It makes shopping a weekly challenge to defy the check-out clerk to ring up your total amount past your budget.

You will not have to spend long periods of time alone nor even spend money to get results. One day a week, Sharon does no housework, except cooking. When her twin daughters take their afternoon nap, she takes a leisurely bath. She shampoos and sets her hair and gives herself a manicure and facial. "I can't explain the psychological aspect of doing this. All I can say is I just feel good all over. I don't feel guilty at all. I take this time just for myself." And her husband is appreciative of the fact that she takes continuing pride in her appearance.

Window-shopping; reading; hearing about and seeing ideas for home use such as new recipes, interior design, lawn care, or fashions—all these can spark your imagination. You might like to set aside this time occasionally to keep a personal family journal. When you have your time alone, write down activities you and the family have done or things you have said. In years to come you will, as Mary did, begin to "ponder them in [your] heart" (Luke 2:19a).

Make long-range plans for a flower garden. Start with a small plot and develop it through the years. Purchase family journals and seed catalogs. Study all sources of horticultural information. Betty has a special section of her lawn for wild flowers. She goes into the woods in early spring and fall and finds various species that could never be found in a store.

There is a verse by Margaret Elizabeth Sangster that states, "There's nothing half so pleasant as coming home again." Even after you have left your childhood home to begin your own home, it is good to go back occasionally and spend some time alone with your parents. During a visit when you take your children, there may not be time for casual or personal conversation you would like to share with your parents. It also benefits your own family to do without mom for a day or two.

## TAKE TIME WITH OTHERS

You may have the kind of personality that desires to relax alone, but at other times it may be equally exciting to spend time with others. There are many activities available to mothers through either organizations or ideas of their own.

A popular and new way to engage in group activities is through crafts. Louise, who has a preschool child, is a creative person. She began talking to other mothers and found they had interests similar to hers. Some of the women had always wanted to work with their hands but felt they were not capable. She very quickly put an end to their misgivings by creating *The Crafty Six*. She began by setting up a work area in her home. While her child napped, the mothers created. The women met once a week, always having a project in mind. Each one bought her own material, or else Louise bought the supplies and each person shared expenses.

In nine months they had made gingham floral arrangements, terrariums, plaques, eyeglass cases, antiqued plastic flowers, ecology boxes (they sawed their own boards), made stuffed strawberries of red dotted swiss material and placed them in apothecary or old fruit jars, and used telephone insulators to make candle holders. The city librarian heard of their work and asked them to display it at the public library, along with arts and crafts books that are available to the public. In the display they placed photographs of the *Crafty Six* at work.

At Christmas they invited their husbands to a party. They planned games, prizes, and refreshments. At the end of the nine months, Louise was honored by the other members by being taken out to lunch. Their group disbanded during the summer months since most of them had school children.

Another foursome organized the *Arty Party Girls*. This group met under similar circumstances which grew out of a need to get away from daily routines and to become completely absorbed in creating and communicating with other young adults. One of the four would attend a demonstration such as making corn husk dolls, using the technique of dip 'n' drape, or decoupage. That person would then go back to the group and teach them how each craft was done.

They became so involved with their work they decided to have a Christmas Open House to sell their work. Each room cleverly displayed their creations and certainly reflected the fun they had in doing this. Some of the more popular items were cross-stitched baby sheets, stuffed animals, antiqued tin cup candles, appliquéd towels and washcloths, and small calico bags of spices attached to a piece of twine to be hung in the kitchen.

When everything was ready, the guests began coming. While everyone was shopping, refreshments of coffee cake and cookies were served to the "potential" buyers. Everything was so well received they planned to make this an annual event.

These four women had shared many hours together developed lasting friendships through common interests. They then extended their talents to let others enjoy them.

Have a neighborhood Christmas Coffee. Ask each woman to bring a coffee cake, cookies, or candy along with its recipe. Place the recipe by each dish. Have blank recipe cards and pens available for the guests to write down the recipes they specially like. Get a circular response started by having each neighbor tell something interesting about herself. This can range from "How did you meet your husband?" to "What was your most embarrassing moment?" They may want to tell something about their children. Any way to get the women better acquainted!

Dorothy wanted to teach the almost extinct art of quilting. She began a class of her own. After a few months the mothers had made four beautiful quilts. They decided to give them to a home for the aged.

Betty's husband realized how serious she was about china painting. She took opportunities to study techniques from various teachers. Her husband built her an attractive studio in their home, and now Betty shares her knowledge with all ages.

Jane had majored in art; but since she had a young family, she did not want to have a job that would take her away from her children. She and her husband designed a very pleasant art studio; and now she teaches tole painting, oils, water colors, and acrylics.

Check into the possibilities of taking tennis, bowling, swimming, or ice skating lessons through a YMCA or other community services. Many cities offer evening adult education courses for sewing, ceramics, oils, typing, shorthand, cooking, nurse's aid, speed reading, and even simple mechanics. These give you opportunities to develop your talents and are excellent ways to get acquainted with other people.

Whether you feel a need to spend time with God, alone, or with others, will determine your effectiveness as a useful, stimulating young woman because indeed your "price is far above rubies" (Prov. 31:10b).

# Take Time for Each Other

*And the Lord God said, It is not good that the man should be alone; I will make him an help meet for him.*

*And the Lord caused a deep sleep to fall upon Adam, and he slept: and he took one of his ribs, and closed up the flesh instead thereof;*

*And the rib, which the Lord God had taken from man, made he a woman, and brought her unto the man.*

*And Adam said, This is now bone of my bones, and flesh of my flesh: she shall be called Woman, because she was taken out of Man.*

*Therefore shall a man leave his father and his mother and shall cleave unto his wife: and they shall be one flesh.–Gen. 2:18, 21-24*

Can you remember when you and your husband said your vows to each other on your wedding day, or were you so exhausted and nervous that the promises you made seem vague? Did your minister remind you that you would have to work at refining your marriage through the years, that you would always keep in mind your promises, and the only way your vows would be broken would be by death?

Look at the wedding band on your finger. Let it

remind you of the promises you made: "to love and to cherish, in sickness and in health, for richer for poorer, for better for worse, as long as you both shall live."

From the first day of marriage you have had time to show your love to each other in numerous ways. You enjoyed your good health and took care of each other if either of you was sick. It really didn't matter if your income was small; you had each other; you were sharing life together. You saw good and bad traits in each other that you had not detected before your marriage, but you worked hard at accepting and respecting each other as individuals.

Later, because of your love, you wanted a child to make your union complete. You had so much fun shopping, fixing your baby's room, choosing a name, and going to parenthood classes together. Your husband helped you watch your diet and encouraged you to keep up with your exercises. You packed your suitcase exactly when "the book" told you to; you timed your labor pains, and then you took that trip to the hospital when you were certain it was time to go. "You have a fine, healthy, baby." You counted the fingers and toes and took a long awesome survey of your completed miracle. You could not find words to thank God for seeing you safely through childbirth.

The first day you were home from the hospital, you began to realize how much time it took to care for your baby. Your new routine tired you and you lost sleep. There were days when an attempted schedule was impossible. You and your husband had such little time for each other. Facing the issue, you began to feel that if you were to continue to mature in your marriage you would have to start taking time not only with your child, but also with your husband.

One of the most essential elements in any successful marriage is the ability to find time to talk with each other. This may not always be a planned time; but if you feel a need to discuss a special purchase, project, trip, family need, or whatever need arises, it takes two to discuss it in order to come to a conclusion.

Be determined to have fifteen minutes every day with each other, and let nothing interfere. You may feel a short time such as this is hardly worth your attention; but after faithfully practicing this a few days, you will begin to look forward to it in order to share your hopes, dreams, discouragements, and uncertainties. Encourage each other in your various roles. Be generous in complimenting each other as wife and husband, mom and dad, homemaker and provider. Some of your conversation could easily turn into natural, private devotions together. It is not necessary to wait until the time you have set aside for your daily devotions; do it then if the need is there. Define your priorities with each other. Yes, you need much time with the children—both of you—but you must not neglect your time together. Try to define the atmosphere you feel in your home. Is it relaxed and happy, or unhappy and angry? What are some activities you are doing in your home that are effective living devices? What are other areas that need improving?

You may have something bothering you. It may not amount to more than the fact that you feel your husband wears the wrong tie and the wrong colored shoes with a certain outfit, or "Could you please start putting your dirty socks in the hamper?" You may learn through conference that you have been fixing that easy tuna casserole too often or you have a habit of leaving the car windows down even though there is a forecast of rain. Most couples can laugh at these pet peeves if they are brought out into the open. You can find humor in almost anything if you try. You can come to a workable solution as long as you talk with each other.

Enjoy each other's company. You may not have anything special to discuss; you just have a desire to have time with each other. Enlist the services of a reliable baby-sitter or trade baby-sitting hours with friends. Then go out for an evening meal or to a good movie, or both. It is amazing what three uninterrupted hours with each other will reveal to both of you. It can enrich your marriage.

Jackie and Tom like to perfect their golf game with each other. They may not get their lowest scores when they go together, but it is more fun. Other athletically inclined couples join bowling leagues, play tennis, go bike riding, swimming, skiing, or fishing. If you are not interested in the sport of fishing, but your husband is, go with him anyway; take a good book along or answer correspondence while your husband fishes. You and your husband may find pleasure in developing your lawn or planting a small flower or vegetable garden.

From the beginning of their marriage Betty was interested in antiques, but her husband was not. When she found an antique china cabinet she wanted very badly, she withheld a small amount of her grocery money each week until she was able to purchase the cabinet. She completely restored it and then presented it for her husband to see. He was impressed. Over a period of time he became equally as interested as she. For their vacations they traveled to New England to purchase items for their house. Today, their home is completely furnished with the "fruits of their labors." It is meaningful to them because they shared in this project together. You may find it satisfying to work at developing an interest in each other's ideas through the years.

Time together may not involve leaving the house. Your child may go to bed early in the evenings. After he is asleep, play table games. Since Don and Sharon sing at many public functions, they use their evenings to practice their music. Do some of the walls in your home need painting or repapering? Take the strain off your budget by doing it yourselves. Anything is more enjoyable when you are doing it with someone.

Your husband enjoys being fussed over. Surprise him with breakfast in bed. Pull up a chair and have some quiet conversation while he eats—he may reverse the procedure some day. Have a flower delivered by the florist with a personal note attached. You can find many finishes to the phrase "I love you because. . . ." Pin it to his pillow; tape it on his mirror; place it in his suit pocket; on the steering wheel of the car; in his suitcase if he travels much in his vocation, or in his lunch if he carries it to work. Perhaps you think you cannot write down your warmest thoughts. It may surprise you to know there are beautiful cards published that convey love in simple verse. Read them to find the one that says what you feel. Be creative. In your wildest dreams what would you like to do with or for that "cherished" mate? Do it. One principle remains constant: get together, talk together, enjoy life together. It isn't necessary to spend money in order to enjoy each other's company. Walk through a luxurious furniture store and dream; sit on a park bench; get in a boat and drift along. "Commit thy way unto the Lord; trust also in him; and he shall bring it to pass (Ps. 37:5). God will help you succeed, but you must help Him by taking time with each other.

Have you ever thought of doing something unique on your wedding anniversary? Here is an idea that any husband will accept as a memorable gift. As you will notice, it will take some planning on your part.

A week before your anniversary make arrangements for a family friend or that faithful baby-sitter to care for your child. Make sure he feels secure and comfortable with the person whom you choose. Without your husband's knowledge, make a motel reservation. A day or two before your anniversary ask him to keep that special evening free. When he comes home from work that day, have the suitcase in hand; meet him at the door and escort him back to the car. First, take him to a nice restaurant for dinner. He will be wondering all the time about the suitcase. Drive him to the motel; check in and the evening is yours—together. Ask him to repeat the marriage vows with you and exchange your love with each other. A renewal of love is a very lasting element between a husband and his wife. The next morning have an early breakfast out. Before you arrive home, let your husband know once more that he meets your every expectation as a husband.

At another anniversary, tape a special message. Quote love poems and pray about the dreams you have as his wife. Give this to him as a gift and have him listen to it in privacy.

Your sexual relationship must remain alive and meaningful. It is your highest form of love for each other. God made it so.

> The husband must always give his wife what is due her, and the wife too must do so for her husband. The wife does not have the right to do as she pleases with her own body; the husband has his right to it. In the same way the husband does not have the right to do as he pleases with his own body; the wife has her right to it. You husbands and wives must stop refusing each other what is due, unless you agree to do so just for awhile, so as to have plenty of time for prayer, and then to be together again, so as to keep Satan from tempting you because of your lack of self-control.
> –I Cor. 7:3-5
>
> Husbands, love your wives, even as Christ also loved the church, and gave himself for it . . . So ought men to love their wives as their own bodies. He that loveth his wife loveth himself. –Eph. 5:25, 28

Both of you realize this need even though there are days that are extremely tense. Sometimes it is difficult to find time for this necessary element in marriage. If your schedule has been unusually busy, your child has demanded more attention and you are physically exhausted, tell your husband. Share in the work responsibilities until things get back to normal, cooperating with each other so there will be time to continue and enjoy this aspect of your marriage.

All married couples need to have wholesome friendships with other couples. After a good rapport has been established, be open with each other. The conversation may end with descriptions of the children's teething, how they are having trouble sleeping, how it has been one of those days, or "that child has gotten into everything today." At other times have some good games on hand. Get some competition going between the husbands and wives.

Elect yourself as hostess and have couples over during the holidays. Plan everything with your husband—menu, table decorations, entertainment, even the soft background music and candlelight. You can count on your husband to come in handy for those last-minute details. Have carry-in meals with other friends. Have a definite menu planned or ask everyone to bring a favorite food. You might suggest a salad dinner or have only desserts over coffee and conversation. Invite your friends over for a late Saturday breakfast. If your child is old enough he will be entertained by cartoons on television while you are serving the meal. This is a good way to begin the day in a leisurely and delightful fashion.

Plan an all-day float trip; enjoy the sunshine and water; laugh together. At the close of the day, have a wiener roast around a campfire. Hold hands and form a circle. Thank God for the privilege of having these kinds of days with Christian friends.

Pray. Pray together. You and your husband realized from the very first day of your lives together that your union could be successful only with God's support. There is always a time in every day that a husband and wife can join hands and pray for each other, their young family, and others. From the moment you accepted the responsibility that goes with the wedding vows, you joined your lives together. This union is kept alive through prayer and hard work. On the days when outward circumstances in home living seem to fall apart and your plans don't develop, you are assured that "the peace of God, which passeth all understanding shall keep your hearts and minds through Christ Jesus" (Phil. 4:7).

Dear Lord,

How can I show my husband how much I truly love him? It seems that I expect so much from him—when to show me attention, when to leave me alone. I think he should know when I am tired, upset, lonely; when I need a change of pace. I enjoy hearing, "I love you," "You're a good mother," "You do a good job with the budget," "You look great." I feel love in many ways. I feel it when I have my family together at a meal, while we're enjoying a movie, watching our child play, or quietly watching him while he sleeps. I love my husband for taking so much time with our child even when I know he is tired, too.

We are one—You have made our union possible. All of this has happened because You, in Your providence, saw fit for us to share this life together.

Jesus, thank You for my husband. This life is a happier one for me because in Your master plan You decided we were to live out our lives together. It takes time to make a good marriage. Please help us. In Jesus' name,

Amen.

"Whoso findeth a wife findeth a good thing, and obtaineth favour of the Lord" (Prov. 18:22).